NorthStar

Focus on Reading and Writing

Introductory

John Beaumont

SERIES EDITORS
Frances Boyd
Carol Numrich

D1122224

NorthStar: Focus on Reading and Writing, Introductory

Pearson Education, 10 Bank Street, White Plains, NY 10606

Vice president, director of publishing: Allen Ascher
Editorial director: Louisa Hellegers
Senior development manager: Penny Laporte
Senior development editor: Carolyn Viola-John
Development editor: Debbie Sistino
Vice president, director of design and production: Rhea Banker
Executive managing editor: Linda Moser
Senior production manager: Alana Zdinak
Production editor: Lynn Contrucci
Director of manufacturing: Patrice Fraccio
Senior manufacturing buyer: Dave Dickey
Cover design: Rhea Banker
Cover illustration: Robert Delaunay, "Formes circulaires, soleil no. 2" 1912. L & M
    Services B. V. Amsterdam 20010804
Text design: Delgado Design, Inc.
Text composition: ElectraGraphics, Inc.
Photo and art credits: **p. 7**, The Friendship Page (www.friendship.com.au); **pp. 19–21**, ©
    The Estate of Keith Haring; **p. 22**, The Alliance of the Guardian Angels, Brooklyn, NY;
    p. 26, © The Estate of Keith Haring; **p. 38**, © Rob Lewine/The Stock Market; **pp. 49,
    50, 53, 56**, The Alliance of the Guardian Angels, Brooklyn, NY; **p. 59**, DAREarts
    Foundation, Inc., Toronto, Ontario, Canada; **p. 62**, The Alliance of the Guardian
    Angels, Brooklyn, NY; **p. 75**, Blockbuster name, design, and related marks are
    trademarks of Blockbuster, Inc. © 2001, Blockbuster, Inc. All rights reserved; **pp. 91,
    97**, © Bettmann/CORBIS; **p. 114**, © Massimo Mastrorillo/The Stock Market; **p. 116**,
    New York City subway logo a trademark of the Metropolitan Transportation
    Authority, used with permission. London Underground logo used with permission,
    London's Transport Museum; **p. 121**, Courtesy of the author; **p. 126**, © Brook
    Kraft/Corbis Sygma; **p. 128**, Bettmann/CORBIS; **p. 141**, New Jersey State Lottery,
    Lawrenceville, NJ
Illustrations: Dusan Petricic, pp. 1, 105, 107, 133, 139; Gary Torrisi, pp. 67, 83, 87, 89,
    101; Deborah White, pp. 35, 47, 146, 147; Jill Wood, pp. 41, 126, 140, 143
Text credits: see page 168.

Library of Congress Cataloging-in-Publication Data

Beaumont, John
    NorthStar. Focus on reading and writing, introductory / John Beaumont ; series editors,
Frances Boyd, Carol Numrich.
        p. cm.
    Includes index.
    ISBN 0-201-61981-4
    1. English language—Textbooks for foreign speakers. I. Title: Focus on reading and
writing, introductory. II. Boyd, Frances Armstrong. III. Numrich, Carol. IV. Title.

PE1128 .B41 2001
428.2'4—dc21

                                                                            2001045767

1 2 3 4 5 6 7 8 9 10—CRK—06 05 04 03 02 01

CONTENTS

Introduction   v

1 THE FRIENDSHIP PAGE   1

Theme: Friendship
Reading One: *The Friendship Page Is Three Years Old!*   6
Reading Two: *Friendship Quotes*   10
Grammar: Questions with *Be*   14
Style: The Sentence   15

2 ART FOR EVERYONE   19

Theme: The Arts
Reading One: *Art for Everyone*   23
Reading Two: *Looking at Art*   26
Grammar: The Simple Past of *Be*   29
Style: Commas   32

3 WHAT'S IT WORTH TO YOU?   35

Theme: Special Possessions
Reading One: *My Secret*   38
Reading Two: *Collecting Today for Tomorrow*   40
Grammar: The Simple Present   44
Style: The Paragraph   46

4 STRENGTH IN NUMBERS   49

Theme: Strength in numbers
Reading One: *Urban Angels*   52
Reading Two: *Two Real Angels*   56
Grammar: Pronouns and Possessive Adjectives   60
Style: Writing a Personal Letter   63

5 GOING OUT OF BUSINESS 67

Theme: Business
Reading One: *The Death of the Family-Owned Video Store?* 71
Reading Two: *Did You Know?* 75
Grammar: *There is/There are* 80
Style: Describing a Place Using Spatial Order 83

6 FLYING HIGH AND LOW 87

Theme: Famous People
Reading One: *Lindbergh Did It!* 91
Reading Two: *Timeline of Lindbergh's Life* 94
Grammar: The Simple Past 98
Style: Time Order 101

7 ARE WE THERE YET? 105

Theme: Driving Problems
Reading One: *Looking for Traffic Solutions* 109
Reading Two: *Transportation Changes How We Do Business* 111
Grammar: Comparative Adjectives 115
Style: Writing about Similarities 118

8 FULL HOUSE 121

Theme: Family
Reading One: *Seven Tiny Miracles* 125
Reading Two: *The Dionne Quintuplets* 128
Grammar: Making Predictions with *be going to* 133
Style: *Because* 135

9 IT'S YOUR LUCKY DAY 139

Theme: Money
Reading One: *Sorry, Mom!* 143
Reading Two: *Joe and Bonnie Put in Their Two Cents* 146
Grammar: *Should*, for Advice 151
Style: Expressing an Opinion 153

Answer Key 157

INTRODUCTION

NorthStar is an innovative five-level, integrated skills series for learners of English as a Second or Foreign Language. The series is divided into two strands: listening/speaking and reading/writing. There are five books in each strand, taking students from the Introductory to the Advanced level. The two books at each level explore different aspects of the same contemporary themes, which allows for reinforcement of both vocabulary and grammatical structures. Each strand and each book can also function independently as a skills course built on high-interest thematic content.

NorthStar is designed to work alongside Longman's *Focus on Grammar* series, and students are referred directly to *Focus on Grammar* for further practice and detailed grammatical explanations.

NorthStar is written for students with academic as well as personal language goals, for those who want to learn English while exploring enjoyable, intellectually challenging themes.

NORTHSTAR'S PURPOSE

The *NorthStar* series grows out of our experience as teachers and curriculum designers, current research in second-language acquisition and pedagogy, as well as our beliefs about language teaching. It is based on five principles.

Principle One: In language learning, making meaning is all-important. The more profoundly students are stimulated intellectually and emotionally by what goes on in class, the more language they will use and retain. One way that classroom teachers can engage students in making meaning is by organizing language study thematically.

We have tried to identify themes that are up-to-date, sophisticated, and varied in tone—some lighter, some more serious—on ideas and issues of wide concern. The forty-nine themes in *NorthStar* provide stimulating topics for the readings and the listening selections, including why people like dangerous sports, the effect of food on mood, an Olympic swimmer's fight against AIDS, experimental punishments for juvenile offenders, people's relationships with their cars, philanthropy, emotional intelligence, privacy in the workplace, and the influence of arts education on brain development.

Each corresponding unit of the integrated skills books explores two distinct topics related to a single theme as the chart below illustrates.

Theme	Listening/Speaking Topic	Reading/Writing Topic
Insects	Offbeat professor fails at breeding pests, then reflects on experience	Extract adapted Kafka's "The Metamorphosis"
Personality	Shyness, a personal and cultural view	Definition of, criteria for, success

Principle Two: Second-language learners, particularly adults, need and want to learn both the form and content of the language. To accomplish this, it is useful to integrate language skills with the study of grammar, vocabulary, and American culture.

In *NorthStar,* we have integrated the skills in two strands: listening/speaking and reading/writing. Further, each thematic unit integrates the study of a grammatical point with related vocabulary and cultural information. When skills are integrated, language use inside of the classroom more closely mimics language use outside of the classroom. This motivates students. At the same time, the focus can shift back and forth from what is said to how it is said to the relationship between the two. Students are apt to use more of their senses, more of themselves. What goes on in the classroom can also appeal to a greater variety of learning styles. Gradually, the integrated-skills approach narrows the gap between the ideas and feelings students want to express in speaking and writing and their present level of English proficiency.

The link between the listening/speaking and reading/writing strands is close enough to allow students to explore the themes and review grammar and reinforce vocabulary, yet it is distinct enough to sustain their interest. Also, language levels and grammar points in *NorthStar* are keyed to Longman's *Focus on Grammar* series.

Principle Three: Both teachers and students need to be active learners. Teachers must encourage students to go beyond whatever level they have reached.

With this principle in mind, we have tried to make the exercises creative, active, and varied. Several activities call for considered opinion and critical thinking. Also, the exercises offer students many opportunities for individual reflection, pair- and small-group learning, as well as out-of-class assignments for review and research. An answer key is printed on perforated pages in the back of each book so

the teacher or students can remove it. A teacher's manual, which accompanies each book, features ideas and tips for tailoring the material to individual groups of students, planning the lessons, managing the class, and assessing students' progress.

Principle Four: Feedback is essential for language learners and teachers. If students are to become better able to express themselves in English, they need a response to both what they are expressing and how they are expressing it.

NorthStar's exercises offer multiple opportunities for oral and written feedback from fellow students and from the teacher. A number of open-ended opinion and inference exercises invite students to share and discuss their answers. In information gap, fieldwork, and presentation activities, students must present and solicit information and opinions from their peers as well as members of their communities. Throughout these activities, teachers may offer feedback on the form and content of students' language, sometimes on the spot and sometimes via audio/video recordings or notes.

Principle Five: The quality of relationships among the students and between the students and teacher is important, particularly in a language class where students are asked to express themselves on issues and ideas.

The information and activities in *NorthStar* promote genuine interaction, acceptance of differences, and authentic communication. By building skills and exploring ideas, the exercises help students participate in discussions and write essays of an increasingly more complex and sophisticated nature.

DESIGN OF THE UNITS

For clarity and ease of use, the listening/speaking and reading/writing strands follow the same unit outline given below. Each unit contains from 5 to 8 hours of classroom material. Teachers can customize the units by assigning some exercises for homework and/or skipping others. Exercises in Sections 1–4 are essential for comprehension of the topic, while teachers may want to select among the activities in Sections 5–7.

1. Approaching the Topic

A warm-up, these activities introduce students to the general context for listening or reading and get them personally connected to the topic. Typically, students might react to a visual image, describe a personal experience, or give an opinion orally or in writing.

2. Preparing to Listen/Preparing to Read

In this section, students are introduced to information and language to help them comprehend the specific tape or text they will study. They might read and react to a paragraph framing the topic, prioritize factors, or take a general-knowledge quiz and share information. In the vocabulary section, students work with words and expressions selected to help them with comprehension.

3. Listening One/Reading One

This sequence of four exercises guides students to listen or read with understanding and enjoyment by practicing the skills of (a) prediction, (b) comprehension of main ideas, (c) comprehension of details, and (d) inference. In activities of increasing detail and complexity, students learn to grasp and interpret meaning. The sequence culminates in an inference exercise that gets students to listen and read between the lines.

4. Listening Two/Reading Two

Here students work with a tape or text that builds on ideas from the first listening/reading. This second tape or text contrasts with the first in viewpoint, genre, and/or tone. Activities ask students to explicitly relate the two pieces, consider consequences, distinguish and express points of view. In these exercises, students can attain a deeper understanding of the topic.

5. Reviewing Language

These exercises help students explore, review, and play with language from both of the selections. Using the thematic context, students focus on language: pronunciation, word forms, prefixes and suffixes, word domains, idiomatic expressions, analogies. The listening/speaking strand stresses oral exercises, while the reading/writing strand focuses on written responses.

6. Skills for Expression

Here students practice related grammar points across the theme in both topics. The grammar is practiced orally in the listening/speaking strand, and in writing in the reading/writing strand. For additional practice, teachers can turn to Longman's *Focus on Grammar,* to which *NorthStar* is keyed by level and grammar points. In the Style section, students practice functions (listening/speaking) or rhetorical styles (reading/writing) that prepare them to express ideas on a higher level. Within each unit, students are led from controlled to freer practice of productive skills.

7. On Your Own

These activities ask students to apply the content, language, grammar, and style they have practiced in the unit. The exercises elicit a higher level of speaking or writing than students were capable of at the start of the unit. Speaking topics include role plays, surveys, presentations, and experiments. Writing topics include paragraphs, letters, summaries, and academic essays.

In Fieldwork, the second part of On Your Own, students go outside of the classroom, using their knowledge and skills to gather data from personal interviews, library research, and telephone or Internet research. They report and reflect on the data in oral or written presentations to the class.

AN INVITATION

We think of a good textbook as a musical score or a movie script: It tells you the moves and roughly how quickly and in what sequence to make them. But until you and your students bring it to life, a book is silent and static, a mere possibility. We hope that *NorthStar* orients, guides, and interests you as teachers.

It is our hope that the *NorthStar* series stimulates your students' thinking, which in turn stimulates their language learning, and that they will have many opportunities to reflect on the viewpoints of journalists, commentators, researchers, other students, and people in the community. Further, we hope that *NorthStar* guides them to develop their own viewpoint on the many and varied themes encompassed by this series.

We welcome your comments and questions. Please send them to us at the publisher:

Frances Boyd and Carol Numrich, Editors
NorthStar
Pearson Education
10 Bank Street
White Plains, NY 10606-1951

ACKNOWLEDGMENTS

The author and publisher wish to thank the following reviewers for their helpful suggestions on the manuscript:

Elizabeth Ruíz Esparza Barajas, University of Sonora, Sonora, Mexico; Cristina Carillo, San Luis Potosí, Mexico; Mary Peterson de Sanabria, Pontificia Universidad Javeriana, Santafé de Bogotá, Colombia; Sarah Dietrich, Salem State College, Salem, Massachusetts; Michael DiGiacomo, GEOS Language Institute, New York, New York; Susan Gillette, Minnesota English Center, Minneapolis, Minnesota; Cristina Narvaez Gocher, Universidad Autómoma de San Luis Potosí, San Luis Potosí, Mexico; Kathy Laise, Spokane Work Source, Spokane, Washington; George Murdoch, UAE University, Al Ain, United Arab Emirates; Maria Ordoñez, Universidad de Celaya, Celaya, Mexico; Muge Nure Pehlevan, Yeditepe University, Istanbul, Turkey; Sajida Saeed Tabbara, ELC University of Bahrain, Sakheer, Bahrain.

Working on this project was a tremendous learning experience for me, and I would like to acknowledge some of the individuals who helped along the way.

First and foremost, I would like to thank Carol Numrich, not only for offering me the opportunity to work on this text, but for being an invaluable mentor and friend. Her devotion to teaching and to this project was a genuine inspiration. We all should have teachers like Carol.

Second, I am grateful to Debbie Sistino and Carolyn Viola-John, for the hours of careful editing and for helping me to look at the material with fresh eyes.

I am also indebted to the teachers at the American Language Program, Columbia University, who teach me so much on a daily basis, and especially to Frances Boyd, for her insights and encouragement, to Polly Merdinger for piloting many of the units in this text and for her support at our meetings at the copy machine. I am also grateful to the ALP Level 1 & 2 students, whose feedback was invaluable.

Louisa Hellegers, Penny Laporte and Lynn Contrucci and the staff at Pearson Education also deserve many thanks for their ever-dependable professionalism and enthusiasm. I am particularly grateful to Stacey Hunter and Iris Bodré-Baez, for their help with research and permissions.

Finally, my sincere thanks go to Bronwyn Polson, Frances Sliwa, Marilyn Field, Richard Woodroof, and the countless others who were generous enough to share their stories with me so that I could share them with students and teachers around the world.

This book is for my parents, Urville and Vera, whose lessons I take with me into the classroom each day.

JB

THE FRIENDSHIP PAGE

1 APPROACHING THE TOPIC

A. PREDICTING

Look at the picture. Discuss these questions with the class.

1. Where are the people?
2. What are they doing?
3. The title of this unit is "The Friendship Page." What do you think? What is The Friendship Page?

B. SHARING INFORMATION

Look at the graph. Then, answer the questions.

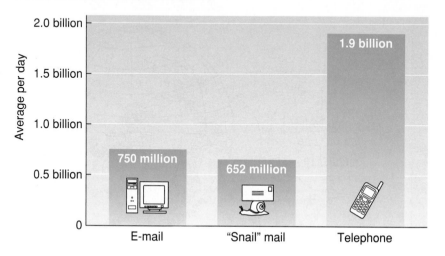

How Americans Communicate

1. Which do Americans use more: e-mail, "snail" mail, or the telephone?

2. Talk to three classmates. How do you and your classmates communicate with friends and family? Complete the chart.

HOW WE COMMUNICATE

	Which do you use the most?			How often?
	E-mail	**"Snail" mail**	**Telephone**	**Every day, sometimes, never, etc.**
You				
Student 1				
Student 2				
Student 3				

2 PREPARING TO READ

A. BACKGROUND

1 *Look at the graph. Then answer the questions.*

Percentage of People Online (on the Internet) in the United States

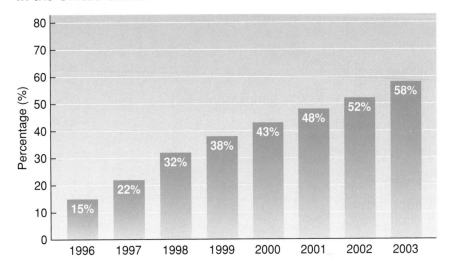

1. What does this graph show?

_____

2. What percentage of people in the United States used the Internet in 1996?

_____

3. What do you think? What percentage of people in the United States will use the Internet in five years?

_____

2 *Look at the chart. Then answer the questions.*

HOW PEOPLE IN THE UNITED STATES USE THE INTERNET

Internet Uses	Percentage of People
Banking	20%
Buying and selling stocks	6%
Doing homework and research for school	35%
E-mailing	96%
Listening to music	35%
Looking for a boyfriend or girlfriend	7%
Making travel plans	47%
Meeting new people	45%
Playing games	38%
Reading the news	51%

1. What are the three most popular uses of the Internet?

_____

_____

2. What are the three least popular uses of the Internet?

_____

_____

3. Do you use the Internet? If yes, how? If not, why not?

_____

_____

B. VOCABULARY FOR COMPREHENSION

Read the sentences. Then circle the definition of the underlined words.

1. Karen and Ellen were friends in elementary school. Today, they are 40 years old, and they still have a strong underlined friendship.

   a. education
   (b.) relationship

2. If you want information about Columbia University in New York City, visit Columbia's website at www.columbia.edu.

   a. a place on the Internet
   b. an office at a university

3. The Internet is very popular today. Many people use it.

   a. liked by many people
   b. difficult for people to use

4. What is your biggest goal for the future? Do you want a good job? A lot of money? A big family?

   a. a problem you have
   b. something you want

5. Take my advice: Work hard today if you have a goal for the future.

   a. an idea or opinion to help someone
   b. money you get from your job

6. My brother tells good jokes. We always laugh when we are together.

   a. a sound you make when you are very sad
   b. a sound you make when something is funny

7. George doesn't have a paying job. He is a volunteer at an elementary school three days a week.

   a. someone who works for no money
   b. someone who works for money

8. I want to be a volunteer in my community. I want to help the people who live near me.

   a. all the people living in one place
   b. all the people you know

9. Dr. Irwin Sarason of the University of Washington says, "Good friends are good for your health." That is a <u>quote</u>. I didn't change his words.

    a. something that is not true
    b. someone's exact words

READING ONE:	The Friendship Page Is Three Years Old!

A. INTRODUCING THE TOPIC

Bronwyn Polson is a young woman from Australia. Bronwyn started The Friendship Page. The Friendship Page is a website on the Internet. Look at part of Bronwyn's website.

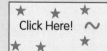 

★ ★ ★ ~ Click Here!

Click Here! ~ ★ ★ ★

The Friendship Page

Fun Facts

"Everything you want to know about friends and friendships."
        —**The Australian Net Guide**

Think about The Friendship Page. What do you think? What is on this website? Check (✓) your ideas.

_____ advice   _____ telephone numbers

_____ humor   _____ pictures

_____ information about Australia   _____ poetry

_____ letters   _____ songs

_____ maps   _____ other: _____

Read "The Friendship Page Is Three Years Old!"

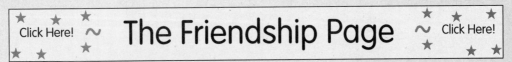

The Friendship Page Is Three Years Old!

1 Happy Birthday to us! The Friendship Page is three years old today.

2 When I was sixteen years old, I wanted to help people in my community. I called people at newspapers and social service organizations,[1] but they just laughed! They said, "You are only sixteen! You are too young to help. There is nothing you can do."

3 So I decided to go online. Age isn't important on the Internet. I learned how to make a website. Then I started The Friendship Page. I chose "friendship" because friendship is important to everyone. I also wanted to make the Internet a friendlier place. My goal is to give something good to the world.

4 Today, I am nineteen years old. The Friendship Page is getting more and more popular. It is very easy to use. Now more than 1,300 people visit this website every day. That's 428,000 people in the first three years!

5 The Friendship Page has fun information about friends and friendship. People can meet new friends. They can get advice about friendship. Also, there are quotes, poetry, songs, writing, humor and more. The poetry page is the most popular.

6 Friends and volunteers help me. The Friendship Page is a lot of work, but we enjoy it.

7 In the future I want The Friendship Page to grow. For example, I want to make a book with quotes about friendship. Money from the book will help to keep The Friendship Page going.

8 If you are interested in friendship and The Friendship Page, please read more!

---

[1] *social service organization*: a group that helps people

B. READING FOR MAIN IDEAS

Read each question. Then circle the best answer.

1. Why did Bronwyn Polson start The Friendship Page?

   a. She wanted to start a business.
   b. She wanted to make new friends.
   c. She wanted to do something good for people.

2. What goal does Bronwyn have for the future?

   a. She wants The Friendship Page to grow.
   b. She wants The Friendship Page to make a lot of money.
   c. She wants people to help her with The Friendship Page.

C. READING FOR DETAILS

Read each sentence. Circle the answer that completes each sentence.

1. Today, Bronwyn Polson is _____ years old.

   a. 16
   b. 19

2. She called people _____ about how to help her community. They just laughed.

   a. in her family
   b. at newspapers

3. Bronwyn's website is _____ to use.

   a. easy
   b. difficult

4. The Friendship Page is _____ website.

   a. a fun
   b. an old

5. There are _____ visits to The Friendship Page each day.

    a. 1,300
    b. 428,000

6. The most popular part is the _____ page.

    a. poetry
    b. quote

7. _____ help Bronwyn with The Friendship Page.

    a. Volunteers and friends
    b. Social service organizations

8. Bronwyn wants to make money from _____.

    a. the website
    b. a book

D. READING BETWEEN THE LINES

*Work with a partner. Read each sentence. What do you think? Write **T** (true) or **F** (false). Then share your answers with the class.*

_____   1. Some adults believe 16-year-old kids are too young to help people.

_____   2. Bronwyn believes the Internet is usually friendly.

_____   3. Bronwyn has a lot of friends.

_____   4. Today, many people think The Friendship Page is a good idea.

_____   5. Bronwyn started The Friendship Page for money.

4 READING TWO: Friendship Quotes

A. EXPANDING THE TOPIC

Read these quotes from The Friendship Page. Use a dictionary for help.

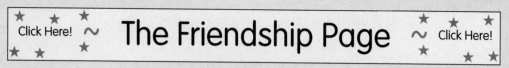

★ ★ ★   **Click Here!** ~ **The Friendship Page** ~ **Click Here!**   ★ ★ ★

Friendship Quotes

a. "I get by with a little help from my friends."—John Lennon

b. "The secret to friendship is being a good listener."—Anonymous

c. "Sometimes your closest friend is your greatest enemy."—sent by Jason Fong

d. "Whenever a friend succeeds, I die a little."—Gore Vidal

e. "The best mirror is an old friend."—George Herbert

Match each quote with its meaning. Write the letter of each quote on the line.

_____ 1. Sometimes someone you think is a friend really is not your friend at all.

_____ 2. If you want to be a good friend, you need to listen to your friends.

_____ 3. You can see yourself in your old friends.

_____ 4. When one of my friends does well, I feel jealous.

a 5. My friends help me live.

B. LINKING READINGS ONE AND TWO

*Look at Reading One again. Then read the quotes from Reading Two. Do you think Bronwyn Polson agrees with each quote? Check (✓) **agree** or **disagree**. Share your answers with a partner.*

	Agree	Disagree
1. "I get by with a little help from my friends."	——	——
2. "The secret to friendship is being a good listener."	——	——
3. "Sometimes your closest friend is your greatest enemy."	——	——
4. "Whenever a friend succeeds, I die a little."	——	——
5. "The best mirror is an old friend."	——	——

5 REVIEWING LANGUAGE

A. EXPLORING LANGUAGE

1 *Work with a partner. First read the three definitions below. Then look at the list of words on page 12. Find them in Readings One and Two. Put each word into the correct group: nouns, adjectives, or verbs. Write the word in the chart.*

Definitions

A **noun** is a person, place, thing, or idea (*woman, school, car,* or *happiness*).

An **adjective** tells something about a noun (a *tall* woman, a *good* school, a *blue* car).

A **verb** shows action (*speak, walk, like*) or being (*be, become*).

~~advice~~	jealous	see
die	laugh	succeed
difficult	little	think
easy	mirror	volunteer
enemy	old	want
friend	poetry	website
friendship	popular	write
fun	secret	young
goal		

NOUNS	ADJECTIVES	VERBS
advice		

2 *Choose one noun, one adjective, and one verb from the chart above. Write a sentence for each.*

1. _____

2. _____

3. _____

B. WORKING WITH WORDS

Look at Reading One again. Then fill in the blanks with one of the words from the list.

advice	online	volunteers
friendship	poetry	website
~~goal~~	popular	young
laughed	quotes	

Bronwyn Polson's _____*goal*_____ is to do something good for
                              1.

the world. She believes that _____ is important to
                                      2.

everyone.

At first, Bronwyn called newspapers and social service organizations,

but they just _____ at her. They thought she was too
                      3.

_____ to help.
        4.

She decided to go _____. She started a
                          5.

_____ called The Friendship Page. It offers information
        6.

and _____ about friendship. The _____
          7.   8.

page is the most _____ part. More than 1,300 people visit
                        9.

The Friendship Page every day. _____ help Bronwyn with
                                        10.

The Friendship Page. It is a lot of work, but she enjoys the work very

much. In the future she wants to make a book with _____
                                                          11.

about friendship.

6 SKILLS FOR EXPRESSION

A. GRAMMAR: Questions with *Be*

1 *Read the questions (Q) and answers (A).*

1. Q: Is The Friendship Page a website?
   A: Yes, it is. It is a website about friendship.
2. Q: Who is Bronwyn Polson?
   A: She is a young woman from Australia.
3. Q: Am I too young to help?
   A: No, you aren't.
4. Q: How old is The Friendship Page?
   A: It is three years old.

Now answer these questions.

◆ Where are the verbs in the questions? Underline the verbs.
◆ Where are the verbs in the answers? Underline the verbs.

FOCUS ON GRAMMAR

See the present of *Be* in *Focus on Grammar,* Introductory.

Questions with *Be*

	Verb Subject
1. For *yes/no* questions, use: the verb *be* + subject	**Is The Friendship Page** a website?
You can answer a *yes/no* question with a short answer.	**Yes, it is.**
Don't use contractions in short answers with *yes*.	**Am I** too young to help? **Yes, you are**. **No, you're not.** **No, you aren't.**
2. For *wh-* questions, use: *Wh-* word + *be* + subject	**Who is** Bronwyn Polson? **What is** The Friendship Page? **When is** your birthday? **Where are** they from? **How old is** The Friendship Page?

2 Write questions about The Friendship Page. Then give your questions to a partner. Ask your partner to write the answers.

1. The Friendship Page / a website?   <u>Is The Friendship Page a website?</u>

2. How old / The Friendship Page? _____

3. Who / Bronwyn Polson? _____

4. Bronwyn / from England? _____

5. Where / Bronwyn / from? _____

6. How old / you? _____

7. Where / you / from? _____

8. Who / your best friends? _____

Your partner's answers

1. <u>Yes, it is.</u> _____

2. _____

3. _____

4. _____

5. _____

6. _____

7. _____

8. _____

B. STYLE: The Sentence

1 Read the paragraph. Then answer the question.

I decided to go online. Age isn't important on the Internet. I learned how to make a website. Then I started The Friendship Page. I chose "friendship" because friendship is important to everyone. I also wanted to make the Internet a friendlier place. My goal is to give something good to the world.

How many sentences are there in this paragraph? _____

The Sentence

1. A *sentence* is a group of words that expresses a complete idea.	
2. A sentence must have a subject and a verb.	Subject Verb **Bronwyn is** a university student. Subject Verb **Volunteers help** with The Friendship Page. Subject Verb **I want** to make a book about friendship.
3. The first word in a sentence must begin with a capital letter.	**T**he website offers information and advice. **F**riendship is important to everyone.
4. Use a period at the end of a sentence.	The Friendship Page has fun information**.**
Use a question mark at the end of a question.	Is age important on the Internet**?**
Use an exclamation point at the end of a sentence with strong feeling.	The Friendship Page is three years old**!**

2 *Read the sentences. Underline the subjects once and the verbs twice. Add punctuation (a period, a question mark, or an exclamation point) at the end of each sentence.*

What Is Tintota____

Tintota is another website about friendship____ It's great____ Friends chat together and help each other on this website____ Warren and Sylvia Roff-Marsh started Tintota____ Like Bronwyn Polson, they live in Australia____ Friendship is important to them, too____

Do you want more information about Tintota____ Visit Tintota's website at www.tintota.com.

3 *Write three sentences about yourself on a piece of paper. Then write three sentences about a friend or a classmate. Begin each sentence with a capital letter. End each sentence with a period.*

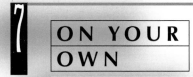

ON YOUR OWN

A. WRITING TOPICS

Choose one of the following writing topics. Use some of the vocabulary, grammar, and style from this unit.

1. Bronwyn Polson has a goal. She wants to help people. She wants people to learn about friendship. Do you have a goal? Write three to five sentences about your goal. Begin with: "In the future I want to . . ."

2. Do you have friends or family members who live far away? How do you communicate with them? By e-mail? By "snail" mail? On the telephone? Why? Write five sentences about communicating with these people.

3. Describe one of your good friends. Who is this person? Why are you friends? Look at the list. Check (✔) the most important qualities of your friend. Use your dictionary for help. Write five or more sentences about your friend.

Qualities of a Good Friend

____ funny

____ good-looking

____ helpful

____ honest

____ intelligent

____ patient

____ popular

____ talkative

your idea(s):

_____

_____

_____

B. FIELDWORK

Learn about the three most important qualities in a friendship.

1. Ask four people about friendship. Ask: "What are the three most important qualities of a good friend?" Write their answers on the lines.

_____
(name)

1. _____
2. _____
3. _____

_____
(name)

1. _____
2. _____
3. _____

_____
(name)

1. _____
2. _____
3. _____

_____
(name)

1. _____
2. _____
3. _____

2. What did most people say? What are the three most important qualities?

a. _____

b. _____

c. _____

3. Write your answers to question 2 on a large piece of paper. Put your paper on the wall of your classroom. Compare your answers and your classmates' answers. What did most people say? Write the qualities here. Are you surprised?

a. _____

b. _____

c. _____

4. Visit The Friendship Page at www.friendship.com.au. Check the Friendship Survey. Are your top three answers similar or different?

ART FOR EVERYONE

© The Estate of Keith Haring

1 APPROACHING THE TOPIC

A. PREDICTING

Look at the picture. Discuss these questions with the class.

1. What is the man doing?
2. Where is he?
3. Read the title of the unit. What does "Art for Everyone" mean?

B. SHARING INFORMATION

Work with a partner. Look at the two pictures. Answer the questions below. Then share your answers with the class.

Picture 1

Picture 2

	PICTURE 1	PICTURE 2
1. What do you see in each picture?		
2. Which picture is more interesting to you? Why?		
3. Give each picture a name or title.		

PREPARING TO READ

A. BACKGROUND

1 *Read the paragraph.*

© The Estate of Keith Haring

Pop Shop NYC logo

The man in the picture on page 19 is Keith Haring. Haring was an American artist. He wanted everyone to share his art.

Haring opened the Pop Shop in New York City in 1986. He opened another Pop Shop in Tokyo, Japan in 1988. Today only the Pop Shop in New York is still open.

The Pop Shop sells pins, pens, watches, pictures, books, T-shirts, ties, toys, and more! Everything has Keith Haring's art on it.

*Now read the sentences. Circle **T** (true) or **F** (false).*

1. The Pop Shop is a restaurant.	T	F
2. You can make art at the Pop Shop.	T	F
3. There were two Pop Shops in 1988.	T	F
4. Today there is only one Pop Shop.	T	F

2 *Have you seen Keith Haring's art before? If so, where?*

B. VOCABULARY FOR COMPREHENSION

Read the words and their definitions in the box. Then complete each sentence with one of the words.

---

ad: short for *advertisement*; words or pictures that make you want to buy something

drawing: a picture made with a pencil or pen

energetic: very active

famous: someone or something that most people know

gallery: a place to look at and buy art

graffiti: pictures and writing on public walls and buildings

museum: a place to look at (but *not* to buy) art

painting: a picture made with paint

public: for everyone to see or use

sculpture: art made with stone, wood, or metal

upset: feeling unhappy, angry, or nervous about something

Graffiti

1. Energetic _____ people like to run, dance, and move a lot.

2. Queen Elizabeth II, Mohandas Gandhi, and Nelson Mandela are all _____ people. Most people know them.

3. Go to a _____ if you want to buy a piece of art.

4. The most famous _____ in France is the Louvre. It has many famous works of art.

5. There is an _____ for computers in this magazine. I want to buy a new computer.

6. There is a new _____ library on Main Street. It is for everyone in our city.

7. Leonardo da Vinci's "Mona Lisa" is a very famous _____.

8. Michelangelo's "David" is a very famous _____.

9. Are you OK? What's wrong? You look very _____.

10. Sometimes young people draw _____ on the side of city buildings. Some people get very upset about it.

11. My daughter made a beautiful _____ with her colored pencils. It's a picture of our house.

3

READING ONE: Art for Everyone

A. INTRODUCING THE TOPIC

Read the following timeline about Keith Haring's life. Then answer the question.

KEITH HARING'S LIFE

Year	Event
1958	Haring is born in Kutztown, Pennsylvania.
1978	Haring goes to New York City.
	He studies at the School of Visual Arts.
	He draws graffiti in the subway of New York City.
1979	Haring leaves the School of Visual Arts.
1981	Haring is arrested by the police in New York City for drawing in the subway.
1982	He stops making graffiti.
	He has his first important show at the Tony Shafrazi Gallery in New York City.
1983–1985	Haring works in Europe, Asia, and the United States.
1986	Haring paints a large picture (a mural) on the Berlin Wall.
	He opens the Pop Shop in New York City.
1987	Haring works in Europe, Asia, and the United States.
1988	He opens the Pop Shop in Tokyo, Japan.
1989	Haring starts the Keith Haring Foundation to help children and people with AIDS.
1990	He dies of AIDS.

In your opinion, for how many years was Haring an artist? Write a number in the space below. Then share your answer with two classmates.

Haring was an artist for _____ years.

Read the following interview. Art World *magazine (AW) talked to Edwin T. Ramoran (ER) about the artist Keith Haring. Mr. Ramoran is from the Bronx Museum of the Arts in New York.*

Art for Everyone

1 **AW:**   Mr. Ramoran, what kind of person was Keith Haring?

ER: Haring liked people. He liked parties and dancing. He was very energetic. You can see his energy in his art. His art moves and dances, too.

2 **AW:**   When did Haring become famous?

ER: In 1978, he started to make pictures in the New York City subway. Some people were very upset. They said, "That isn't art. It's graffiti!"

3   But graffiti *is* art. And some people liked his art very much. They started to buy his other drawings, paintings, and sculptures. Then galleries became interested in his art, too. By the mid-1980s, Keith Haring was famous around the world.

4 **AW:**   What is Haring's art about? What does it mean?

ER: People asked Haring, "What is your art about?" He answered, "You decide." His art is funny, energetic, and sometimes angry. It is also political.

5   His art is about education, freedom, and AIDS. These social issues were very important to Haring. His art is also about children. He worked with kids on many projects. For example, he made a large sculpture for a children's hospital in New York.

6 **AW:**   Was Haring different from other artists?

ER: Yes, he was.

7 **AW:**   How was he different?

ER: Haring liked to make art in public places, like the subway. He believed "art is for everyone." First, he was famous for his public art. Later, he became famous in galleries and museums.

8   He was also different because his paintings and drawings were in magazine ads. His art was on other things such as Swatch watches. He also sold his art in the Pop Shop. He used his art in unusual ways to communicate with the world.

9 **AW:**   Is his art still popular?

ER: Yes, it is. Haring died in 1990, but people still feel his energy in his art. Today we can see his art all around the world. Some of the money from his art helps AIDS organizations and children's organizations. His art still helps people.

10 **AW:**   Very interesting. Thank you, Mr. Ramoran.

ER: It was my pleasure.

B. READING FOR MAIN IDEAS

Read each sentence. Circle the answer that completes the sentence.

1. Keith Haring's first drawings were in the _____ of New York City.

   a. subway   **b.** galleries   **c.** museums

2. Haring made art for _____.

   a. museums   **b.** galleries   **c.** people

3. Haring's art was about _____.

   a. social issues   **b.** important cities   **c.** public places

C. READING FOR DETAILS

Complete the sentences with the words below. Use each word only once.

ads   graffiti   public
decide   money   social issues
energy

1. You can see his _____ in his art. It moves.

2. Some people said his work was just _____ and not really art.

3. At first, he was famous for his _____ art.

4. He made _____ for magazines.

5. People asked, "What is your art about?" Haring answered, "You _____."

6. _____, like AIDS and freedom, were important to Haring.

7. Some of the _____ from the Pop Shop goes to AIDS organizations and children's organizations.

D. READING BETWEEN THE LINES

Work with a partner. Why did people like Keith Haring's work? Check (✓) the two most important reasons. Then share your ideas with the class.

In the 1980s, people liked Haring's art because it was _____.

_____ different   _____ happy   _____ young

_____ easy to   _____ new   _____ your idea:
      understand
                 _____ public   _____

_____ energetic

4 READING TWO: Looking at Art

A. EXPANDING THE TOPIC

Here are two more pictures by Keith Haring. Look at them carefully. Then answer the questions.

STOP AIDS

© The Estate of Keith Haring

FREE SOUTH AFRICA

© The Estate of Keith Haring

1. What do you see in these pictures?

2. How are these two pictures similar to the pictures on page 20?

3. How are these two pictures different from the pictures on page 20?

B. LINKING READINGS ONE AND TWO

Look at all of the Haring pictures in this unit again. What important ideas are in Haring's art? Check (✓) the boxes. Then share your answers with the class.

IDEAS IN HARING'S ART	Untitled, 1984 (Picture 1, page 20)	Radiant Baby (Picture 2, page 20)	Pop Shop NYC Logo (page 21)	Stop AIDS (page 26)	Free South Africa (page 26)
Politics					
AIDS					
Love					
Energy					
Freedom					
Children					
Fear					
Other: _____					

REVIEWING LANGUAGE

A. EXPLORING LANGUAGE

1 *Energetic is a positive or good feeling. Angry is a negative or bad feeling. Mark the other words positive (+) or negative (–). Use your dictionary for help.*

_+_ **1.** energetic   ____ **5.** relaxed

_–_ **2.** angry   ____ **6.** sad

____ **3.** happy   ____ **7.** upset

____ **4.** nervous

2 *Look at the Haring pictures on pages 20, 21, and 26 again. How do they make you feel? For each picture, finish this sentence. Use some of the words above.*

This picture makes me feel _____.

B. WORKING WITH WORDS

Read the clues. Complete the crossword puzzle with words from the box.

ads
art
drawings
energy
famous
galleries
graffiti
kids
painter
pop
~~public~~
~~Shop~~
social

Across

1. In 1988, Haring opened the Pop _____ in Tokyo. It closed after one year.

6. He believed "_____ is for everyone."

8. The word _____ is short for "popular."

9. Some people said, "This is not art. It's just _____."

10. Education and freedom are _____ issues.

11. Haring had a lot of _____. You can see it in his art.

12. The word _____ is short for "advertisements."

Down

2. Haring made _____ art. He wanted everyone to see his art.

3. People around the world know Haring. He is a _____ artist.

4. In the early 1980s, Haring made many _____ in the New York City subway.

5. Another word for "children" is _____.

7. A person who paints is a _____.

9. By the mid-1980s, Haring's work was in many art _____ around the world.

6 SKILLS FOR EXPRESSION

A. GRAMMAR: The Simple Past of *Be*

1 *Read the information about Keith Haring on page 30. Then answer the questions.*

AW: Was Haring different from other artists?

ER: Yes, he was.

AW: How was he different?

ER: Haring liked to make art in public places, like the subway. He believed "Art is for everyone." First, he was famous for his public art. Later, he became famous in galleries and museums.

He was also different because his paintings and drawings were in magazine ads. His art was on other things such as Swatch watches. He also sold his art in the Pop Shop. He used his art in unusual ways to communicate with the world.

◆ Underline *was* and *were* in the interview above. How many examples can you find? Write the numbers on the lines.

was _____   *were* _____

◆ When do we use *am*, *is*, and *are*? When do we use *was* and *were*?

The Simple Past of *Be*

<table>
<tr><td>1. The simple past forms of *be* are *was* and *were*.</td><td>Keith Haring **was** an artist.
Social issues **were** important to him.</td></tr>
<tr><td>2. For negative sentences, use:
subject + *was/were* + *not*
The contraction of *was not* is *wasn't* and of *were not* is *weren't*.</td><td>Subject
His art **was not** in museums in the early 1980s.
His paintings **were not/weren't** in museums at first.</td></tr>
<tr><td>3. For *yes/no* questions, use:
was/were + subject

You can answer a *yes/no* question with a short answer.</td><td>Subject
Was Haring different from other artists?
Yes, he was.
Were his drawings always famous?
No, they weren't.</td></tr>
<tr><td>4. For *wh-* questions, use:
Wh- word + *was/were* + subject</td><td>**Who was** Keith Haring?
What was his art about?
How were his pictures different?</td></tr>
</table>

FOCUS ON GRAMMAR

See the past of *Be* in *Focus on Grammar,* Introductory.

2 *Complete each sentence.*

1. Keith Haring and Andy Warhol _____*were*_____ famous artists in the 1980s.

was/were

2. Both Haring and Warhol _____ from Pennsylvania.

was/were

3. Haring and Warhol _____ the same age. Warhol _____ 31 years

wasn't/weren't _____ was/were

   older than Haring.

4. In the 1950s Warhol _____ a commercial artist on Madison Avenue in New York.

was/were

5. By the early 1960s Andy Warhol _____ a famous Pop artist.

was/were

6. Jasper Johns, Robert Rauschenberg, and Roy Lichtenstein _____ also important

wasn't/were

   pop artists.

7. Like Haring's art, Warhol's art _____ controversial.

was/wasn't

8. Warhol _____ a painter, sculptor, writer, and filmmaker.

was/were

9. Keith Haring _____ a painter and a sculptor, but he _____ a writer

was/wasn't _____ was/wasn't

   or a filmmaker.

10. Andy Warhol and Keith Haring _____ good friends in the 1980s.

was/were

3 *Write questions about Keith Haring and his art. Use **was** or **were** in your questions. Then give your questions to a partner. Ask your partner to write the answers.*

1. Who / Keith Haring?   Who was Keith Haring? _____

2. Haring / famous in the 1970s? _____

3. In what city / Haring / born? _____

4. Haring / only a painter? _____

5. his drawings / controversial? _____

6. Where / the two Pop Shops? _____

7. How old / Keith Haring / in 1990? _____

Your partner's answers

1. <u>Keith Haring was an artist in the 1980s.</u>

2. _____

3. _____

4. _____

5. _____

6. _____

7. _____

B. STYLE: Commas

1 *Work with a partner. Read the sentences about Keith Haring's life. Circle the commas. Then answer the question below.*

1. Keith Haring was born on May 4, 1958.

2. Haring lived in Knokke, Belgium in 1987.

3. He liked to paint, draw, and sculpt.

4. Haring's art was funny, but it was also serious.

5. He also made commercial art. For example, he made ads for magazines.

When do we use commas? Look at the sentences again. Then write the numbers of the sentences next to each correct rule below.

Use a comma:

  5   **a.** after words like *For example* and *Finally.*

_____ **b.** in dates.

_____ **c.** to join two small sentences with *and, but,* and *or.*

_____ **d.** to separate the names of cities from the names of the states or countries.

_____ **e.** to separate things in a list.

2 *Read the two paragraphs. Add six commas to each paragraph.*

The Haring Family

Keith Haring was born in Kutztown Pennsylvania. He lived with his mother his father and his three sisters. His sisters' names were Kay Karen and Kristen. Keith liked Kay and Karen but Kristen was probably his favorite. Kristen was the baby in the family. She was 12 years younger than Keith. Keith and Kristen were always good friends.

Tokyo Pop Shop

Haring opened a Pop Shop in Tokyo on January 30 1988. He wanted the Tokyo Pop Shop to be successful but it had many problems. People did not buy Haring's art at the Tokyo Pop Shop because there were cheap copies everywhere. For example it was easy to buy T-shirts pins and posters with "fake" Haring art on them. Finally the Pop Shop in Tokyo closed in 1989.

ON YOUR OWN

A. WRITING TOPICS

Choose one of the following writing topics. Use some of the vocabulary, grammar, and style from this unit.

1. Look at the pictures on pages 20, 21, and 26 again. Choose one picture. Write five or more sentences about this picture. What is in the picture? How does it make you feel?

2. Keith Haring used simple symbols (like babies, animals, and dancers) in his art. Draw a symbol that is important for people today. Write five or more sentences about the symbol.

3. Keith Haring wanted everyone to experience his art. It was "art for everyone." What do you think? Was it art for everyone? Write five or more sentences.

4. The word *controversial* means that people have different opinions about something. Haring's art was controversial, especially in the 1980s. Some people liked it, and some people didn't like it. Look at the pictures on pages 20, 21, and 26 again. Why do you think Haring's art was controversial? Write five or more sentences about Haring and his art.

B. FIELDWORK

These are some artists that Haring knew well. Choose one artist from the list or a different artist. Then follow the steps.

Roy Lichtenstein   Jean-Michel Basquiat
Claes Oldenburg   Francesco Clemente
Robert Rauschenberg   Kenny Scharf
Andy Warhol

1. Learn about this artist. Write five or more sentences about this artist. Answer some of these questions:

   Is the artist still living?
   Was this artist famous?
   Did this person have a good life?
   What kind of art did this person make?
   Was the art controversial?

2. Find one piece of art by this artist. Then write five or more sentences about the piece of art. Answer some of these questions:

   What do you see in the art?
   Do you like his or her art?
   How does it make you feel?

3. Share your writing and the piece of art with a partner. Read your partner's sentences and look at the piece of art. Take notes.

   Artist's name: _____
   What do you know about this artist?
   What do you know about this artist's art?

WHAT'S IT WORTH TO YOU?

1 APPROACHING THE TOPIC

A. PREDICTING

Look at the picture. Discuss these questions with the class.

1. What is the woman holding?
2. Is it old or new?
3. Why does she keep it?

B. SHARING INFORMATION

Do you collect anything? Stamps? Toys? Dolls? Coins? Something else? Do you have a special possession (something special that is yours)? Why do you have it? Ask four classmates about their special collection or possession. Write their answers below.

NAME	COLLECTION/ POSSESSION	WHY?
You		
Student 1		
Student 2		
Student 3		
Student 4		

2 PREPARING TO READ

A. BACKGROUND

Read the paragraphs. Then answer the questions.

Antiques Roadshow is a popular television show in the United States. The show travels to different cities. The guests on the show are regular people. They bring special possessions and collections to the show. Sometimes they bring antiques—old and valuable things, such as art, furniture, or jewelry. The guests tell stories about these things. They ask questions. They want to know if their things are valuable.

This type of show started in England more than 20 years ago. You can see similar television shows in other countries around the world.

1. Is this type of show shown only in the United States?

2. Is there a similar TV show in your country? Do you watch it?

B. VOCABULARY FOR COMPREHENSION

Read the sentences. Then write each underlined word next to the correct definition below.

1. Some television shows are very <u>educational</u>. You can learn a lot if you watch them.

2. This book is 100 years old, but it is still in good <u>condition</u>. It looks new.

3. I will tell you my <u>secret</u> because you are my best friend. Please don't tell anyone!

4. The woman at the jewelry store knows a lot about diamonds. She is a diamond <u>expert</u>.

5. The diamond expert said, "This diamond ring <u>is worth</u> $5,000."

6. Good diamonds are very <u>rare</u>. It is difficult to find big, beautiful ones.

7. My boyfriend gave me these flowers in 1995. I keep them because they have a lot of <u>sentimental value</u>. Today, my boyfriend is my husband.

8. I need three <u>items</u> from the market: bread, cheese, and a bottle of milk.

_____expert_____ **a.** a person with a lot of knowledge and experience with something

_____ **b.** an idea or fact that you do not want other people to know

_____ **c.** having a value in personal feelings or emotions

_____ **d.** helping you to learn

_____ **e.** not common; not often seen

_____ **f.** objects or things

_____ **g.** the form or state of something

_____ **h.** has a value or a price

3

READING ONE: My Secret

A. INTRODUCING THE TOPIC

Dan Stone writes a sports column for the Boston Daily News. *Read the beginning of the sports column. Then, with a partner, answer the question: What is Dan Stone's secret?*

I am a sports writer and I love my job because I love sports, especially football and baseball. But I have a secret.

Every Monday night I watch my favorite TV show. Sometimes the telephone rings, but I don't answer it. I tell my friends that I watch *Monday Night Football,*[1] but that isn't true.

Now read Dan Stone's column.

My Secret

Boston Daily News

Inside Sports

By DAN STONE

1   I am a sports writer and I love my job because I love sports, especially football and baseball. But I have a secret.

2   Every Monday night I watch my favorite TV show. Sometimes the telephone rings, but I don't answer it. I tell my friends that I watch *Monday Night Football,* but that isn't true.

3   My favorite show is more exciting than *Monday Night Football.* It is also very educational. I learn a lot about art and U.S. history every week.

4   Here is my secret: On Monday nights I watch *Antiques Roadshow.* It is a show about antiques and collections. It's great! Fourteen million people watch it every week.

5   The show is simple. The guests on the show are real people. The guests bring in old art, furniture, books, toys, and much, much more. First the guests tell the experts about their items. The stories are the best part of *Roadshow.* Then the experts talk about the items. Finally, the experts say how much the items are worth.

6   One woman, Veronica, had a painting with trees and animals in it. Veronica's grandmother got the picture for free in 1925. The expert looked at Veronica's picture carefully and said, "This is very rare. Thomas Cole is the artist. Cole painted this around 1835. Your painting is worth

---

[1] *Monday Night Football:* professional football game on TV every Monday night

$125,000." Veronica was very surprised. She told the expert, "Wow! That's a lot of money! But I don't really care about the money. I'm going to keep it because it has a lot of sentimental value."

7   I want *Antiques Roadshow* to come to my city. I am ready. I have a baseball signed by Babe Ruth and Jackie Robinson in the 1940s. It's in perfect condition. I also have a baseball card collection. I started the collection when I was a young boy. The autographed baseball and my baseball cards have a lot of sentimental value to me. Maybe they are worth a lot of money, too!

8   And you? Are you ready? Look carefully around your home! You might have something very valuable.

9   So, remember, don't call me on Monday nights. I'm watching "football."

B. READING FOR MAIN IDEAS

*Read each sentence. Check (✓) **True** or **False**. Then write the number of the paragraph where you found the answer.*

	True	False	Paragraph Number
1. Dan Stone watches football on Monday nights.	❑	❑	____
2. People who watch *Antiques Roadshow* can learn a lot.	❑	❑	____
3. *Antiques Roadshow* is a sports show.	❑	❑	____
4. *Antiques Roadshow* buys items from the guests.	❑	❑	____

C. READING FOR DETAILS

Match each question to the correct answer. Then write the number of the paragraph where you found the answer.

_e (2)_   1. What do Stone's friends think he watches on Monday nights?

_____   2. What do people learn about on *Antiques Roadshow*?

_____   3. What do people bring to *Antiques Roadshow*?

_____   4. For Stone, what is the best part of the show?

_____   5. How much is the woman's picture worth?

_____   6. What does Stone want to bring to *Antiques Roadshow*?

a. items from home

b. $125,000

c. art and U.S. history

d. the stories

e. football

f. an autographed baseball and his baseball cards

D. READING BETWEEN THE LINES

In his article Dan Stone said, "Fourteen million people watch it every week." Why is Antiques Roadshow *popular? Check (✓) all the possible answers. Then share your answers with the class.*

Antiques Roadshow is popular because _____.

_____   1. the show is educational

_____   2. people need money

_____   3. the people on the show are funny

_____   4. people remember their family history

_____   5. the stories are interesting

_____   6. the guests are real people

_____   7. your idea: _____

READING TWO: Collecting Today for Tomorrow

A. EXPANDING THE TOPIC

Read these tips from an expert about collecting.

Collecting Today for Tomorrow

Starting a collection is easy. Here are four tips:

TIP 1: Enjoy. Enjoy collecting. Collect things that you are interested in. Collect things that you want to keep for a long time.

TIP 2: Educate yourself. Become an expert. Read a lot. Talk to antiques experts. Ask a lot of questions. Don't worry! Experts love to talk.

TIP 3: Look for the best. Collect things in good condition. For example, an antique toy in "mint," or perfect, condition will be valuable in the future. A similar toy in bad condition will not be as valuable.

TIP 4: Buy rare items. Collect items that are rare. Rare things are more valuable than common things. If the items you collect are rare today, they will be more valuable in the future.

Match each example below with one of the tips on page 40. Write the tip number (1, 2, 3, or 4) on the line.

_____ **a.** First, learn about antique cars. Then, collect them.

_____ **b.** Collecting coins from the 1800s is better than collecting common coins from today.

_____ **c.** If you love Barbie dolls, then collect them.

_____ **d.** Don't buy a stamp for your collection if it is ripped.

ripped

B. LINKING READINGS ONE AND TWO

*Who is asking the question? Check (✓) **Expert** or **Guest**. Then match the questions with the answers.*

Expert	Guest			
❏	☑	_d_	1. Do you watch *Antiques Roadshow* often?	**a.** I paid about $5.
❏	❏	____	2. Is it good to buy a painting by Keith Haring?	**b.** No, buy only the best.
❏	❏	____	3. How much did you pay for it?	**c.** My grandfather was a mail carrier. We collected them together when I was young.
❏	❏	____	4. When did you get this beautiful watch?	**d.** Yes, I do. Every Monday night!
❏	❏	____	5. Do you think my collection is valuable?	**e.** No. It's interesting, but not valuable.
❏	❏	____	6. Is it OK to buy an antique toy in bad condition?	**f.** I got it about 10 years ago.
❏	❏	____	7. Do you plan to sell your old Barbie dolls?	**g.** My father gave it to me.
❏	❏	____	8. Why do you collect stamps?	**h.** No, I don't. They have a lot of sentimental value.
❏	❏	____	9. Who gave you this chair?	**i.** Yes, his art is very collectible.

REVIEWING LANGUAGE

A. EXPLORING LANGUAGE

Remember that a noun is a person, place, thing, or idea. An adjective is a word that describes a noun. Sometimes you can tell if a word is a noun or an adjective by looking at the last letters in the word. Some nouns end in *-tion, -ment,* and *-or.* Some adjectives end in *-al, -able,* and *-ible.*

*Work with a partner. Look for the words below in the Readings. Put the words into two groups: **nouns** or **adjectives**.*

~~collectible~~	education	favorite	rare
collection	educational	guest	secret
collector	excitement	historical	sentimental
common	exciting	history	valuable
condition	expert	item	value

NOUNS	ADJECTIVES
	collectible

B. WORKING WITH WORDS

Complete the sentences on page 43 with the correct words.

condition, valuable

I found some of my childhood toys in my mother's house. I wonder if

any of them are _____ today. They are all in good

1.

_____.

2.

antique, worth

My mother collects _____ jewelry. She has a very old

3.

watch. The watch isn't _____ very much, but she still

4.

really likes it.

collection, collector, collect

I began to _____ stamps when I was ten years old. I

5.

plan to give my _____ to my son when he is ten years old.

6.

I hope he wants to be a stamp _____ like I am.

7.

sentimental, rare, value

This was my grandparents' kitchen table. You can't buy a table like it

today. It is very _____. It isn't a beautiful table, but I keep

8.

it because it has a lot of _____ _____.

9.   10.

expert, favorite, history

My father likes to read about _____. His

11.

_____ subject is the U.S. Civil War. He is an

12.

_____ on the Civil War. He knows a lot about it.

13.

SKILLS FOR EXPRESSION

A. GRAMMAR: The Simple Present

1 *Read these paragraphs from "My Secret." Then answer the questions.*

I am a sports writer and I love my job because I love sports, especially football and baseball. But I have a secret.

Every Monday night I watch my favorite TV show. Sometimes the telephone rings, but I don't answer it. I tell my friends that I watch *Monday Night Football,* but that isn't true.

1. How many verbs are in these paragraphs? Underline them.

2. Which verbs are negative? Circle them.

3. When does the action in these paragraphs happen?
   a. in the past   b. in the present   c. in the future

FOCUS ON GRAMMAR

See the simple present in *Focus on Grammar,* Introductory.

The Simple Present

1. Use the simple present tense for everyday actions or facts.	I **have** a secret. Sometimes the telephone **rings,** but I **don't answer** it.
2. When the subject is *he, she,* or *it,* put an *s* at the end of the regular verbs. Note: *Be* and *have* are irregular.	**She collects** antique jewelry. ***Antiques Roadshow* is** my favorite show. **Dan has** a secret.
3. For negative sentences, use: *do* (or *does*) + *not* + the base form of the verb In speaking and informal writing, use the contractions *don't* and *doesn't.*	Stone **does not watch** football on Mondays. I **do not like** to play golf. Sometimes the telephone rings, but I **don't** answer it.

> **4.** For *yes/no* questions, use:
> *Do* (or *Does*) + subject + the base form of the verb
> Use *do* or *does* in short answers.
>
> **Do diamonds cost** a lot?
> **Yes, they do.**
> **Does Dan Stone watch** football on Mondays?
> **No, he doesn't.**

> **5.** For *wh-* questions, use:
> *Wh-* word + *do* (or *does*) + subject + the base form of the verb
>
> **What do you watch** on Monday nights?
> **Where do you like** to play golf?
> **How much does that car cost?**

2 *Complete this dialogue. Fill in the present tense form of each verb.*

EXPERT: Welcome to *Antiques Roadshow*. What (1) _____do_____ you
_____have_____ (**have**) with you today?

WOMAN: I (2) _____ (**have**) my mother's diamond wedding ring. I love
this ring very much. I (3) _____ (**remember**) my mother when I
(4) _____ (**wear**) it.

EXPERT: (5) _____ you _____ (**wear**) it often?

WOMAN: Yes, I (6) _____ (**do**). I never (7) _____ (**take**) it off.

EXPERT: What (8) _____ you _____ (**know**) about this ring?

WOMAN: My father gave it to my mother in 1912. I (9) _____ (**not/know**)
where he got it. My husband (10) _____ (**not/think**) that it
(11) _____ (**be**) worth a lot of money. (12) _____ it
_____ (**look**) valuable to you?

EXPERT: Well, it (13) _____ (**be**) a beautiful ring, but I have some bad
news. This (14) _____ (**not/be**) a real diamond. It (15)
_____ (**be**) fake. It is worth about $50.

WOMAN: Really? My husband was right! Well, I still (16) _____ (**love**) it.
My husband and I (17) _____ (**plan**) to give it to our daughter.
We (18) _____ (**want**) this ring to stay in our family. It (19)
_____ (**have**) a lot of sentimental value. Thank you very much!

B. STYLE: The Paragraph

1 *Read the paragraph. Then answer the questions below.*

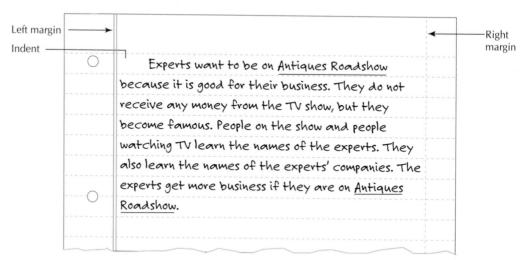

Left margin ⟶
Indent ⟶
Right margin ⟵

Experts want to be on <u>Antiques Roadshow</u> because it is good for their business. They do not receive any money from the TV show, but they become famous. People on the show and people watching TV learn the names of the experts. They also learn the names of the experts' companies. The experts get more business if they are on <u>Antiques Roadshow</u>.

1. What is the main idea of this paragraph? Circle the sentence that has the main idea.

2. Does the writer begin each new sentence on a new line, or does the writer continue on the same line?

3. When does the writer stop and move down to the next line?

The Paragraph

A *paragraph* is a group of sentences that develops one main idea.
The first sentence usually gives the main idea of the paragraph.
Indent the first line of your paragraph. If you use a computer, hit the "tab" button once or hit the space bar five times.
There are two margins on your paper. Write your paragraph between the two margins.
When you write a paragraph, do not start each new sentence on a new line. Continue writing to the right margin.

2 *On a piece of lined paper, write two paragraphs with these sentences. Follow the rules for paragraph form. Your paragraphs will look like the paragraph on page 46.*

Paragraph 1

In 1997, a man named Russ Pritchard was a guest on *Antiques Roadshow.*

He had a large sword.

When he was young, Pritchard found the sword in his new house.

George Juno, an antiques expert, told Pritchard it was an American Civil War sword.

Juno said the sword was very rare and worth $35,000.

Pritchard was very surprised to hear this.

Paragraph 2

On March 31, 2000, there was a story in the newspaper about Pritchard and Juno.

WGBH, a Boston TV station, learned that Pritchard's story was not true.

Pritchard and Juno had made up the story together.

WGBH was very angry because it wants only true stories on *Antiques Roadshow.*

As a result, Juno cannot be on *Antiques Roadshow* in the future.

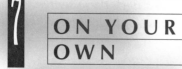

ON YOUR OWN

A. WRITING TOPICS

Choose one of the following topics. Write your answer on a piece of lined paper. Use some of the vocabulary, grammar, and style from this unit.

1. Do you have a special possession or collection? What is it? Why do you keep it? Was it a gift? Does it have sentimental value? Is it worth a lot of money? Write a paragraph about it.

2. Why do people collect things? Write a paragraph with your opinion.

3. Why do people bring items to *Antiques Roadshow*? Do you think they are interested in history and sentimental value? Are they interested in money? Write a paragraph with your opinion.

4. Is there a TV show like *Antiques Roadshow* in your country? If yes, write a paragraph about the show.

B. FIELDWORK

Visit an antiques store.

1. Choose one item in the store. Learn about the item. Take a photograph, if possible. Then write answers to the questions below.

What is it?	Where is it from?
Is it valuable?	How old is it?
What is it worth?	What (material) is it made of?
Is it rare?	Do many people collect this kind of item?

2. Write a paragraph about the item on a piece of lined paper. Use some of your answers to the questions above. Start your paragraph like this: "I learned about an interesting item in an antiques store."

3. Share your writing and photograph with a partner. Read your partner's paragraph. Then answer these questions.

   a. Did the writer indent the first line of the paragraph?
   b. Did the writer use margins correctly?
   c. Which sentences explain why the item is interesting? Underline them.

STRENGTH IN NUMBERS

1 APPROACHING THE TOPIC

A. PREDICTING

Look at the picture. Discuss these questions with the class.

1. Who are the people?
2. What are they wearing?
3. What do they do?
4. Look at the title of the unit. What does "Strength in Numbers" mean?

B. SHARING INFORMATION

Read the list of social issues. Are these problems for young people in your city or town? Rate each social issue from 1 (not a problem) to 4 (a serious problem). Circle the number. Discuss your answers with the class.

Social issues	Not a problem			A serious problem
1. Alcohol	1	2	3	4
2. Drugs	1	2	3	4
3. Finding a job	1	2	3	4
4. Gangs[1]	1	2	3	4
5. Having babies	1	2	3	4
6. Smoking	1	2	3	4
7. Staying in school	1	2	3	4
8. Your idea: _____	1	2	3	4

2 PREPARING TO READ

A. BACKGROUND

Read this information about the Guardian Angels. Then answer the questions on page 51.

The people in the picture on page 49 are Guardian Angels. The Guardian Angels teach people about safety and stopping crime.[2] They want to make life better in their communities.

The man in the center of the picture is Curtis Sliwa. He started the Guardian Angels in 1979. Sliwa and the Guardian Angels look like a gang, but they aren't. They are just people who want to help others.

Today the Guardian Angels are in cities in the United States, Japan, Sweden, England, and Italy.

---

[1] *gangs:* groups of young people who often make trouble

[2] *crime:* an action that is wrong and that can be punished by the law (stealing and killing are crimes)

1. Are the Guardian Angels helpful? Are they dangerous?

2. Does your city have a group like the Guardian Angels? Does it need a group like the Guardian Angels? Why or why not?

B. VOCABULARY FOR COMPREHENSION

Read the sentences. Then match each underlined word with the correct definition.

1. My brother's <u>nickname</u> is Bob. His real name is Robert.

2. Heather is a very <u>positive</u> person. She always has something good to say.

3. Holly is a very <u>generous</u> woman. She always gives her time and money to people who need help.

4. Kelly is in college. Her parents <u>support</u> her. They send her money every month.

5. Young people need to <u>respect</u> old people. Older people can teach us a lot.

6. I was a <u>member</u> of the baseball team in high school.

7. These days many kids are <u>at-risk</u>. Adults need to help these kids stay out of trouble.

8. All parents want their kids to <u>avoid</u> drugs, gangs, and other trouble.

9. Some professional athletes are <u>role models</u> for young people to follow.

10. Sometimes <u>teenagers</u> fight with their parents and their younger brothers and sisters.

11. Life in <u>urban</u> areas like New York City and Hong Kong is different from life in small towns.

_8_ **a.** to stay away from

____ **b.** a person who is in a group or organization

____ **c.** a special name or a short form of your real name

____ **d.** good, helpful, not negative

____ **e.** willing to give money, help, or time

____ **f.** people who are good examples for other people to follow

____ **g.** may have problems in the future

____ **h.** to give money, food, or help to someone

____ **i.** young people from 13 to 19 years old

____ **j.** big-city

____ **k.** to honor, to have a high opinion of

READING ONE: Urban Angels

A. INTRODUCING THE TOPIC

Read the chart. Then complete the activity below.

SOCIAL ISSUES AND PROBLEMS FOR U.S. TEENAGERS

Number of teenagers per month	
883	Start smoking
84,798	Hurt in car accidents involving alcohol
38,159	Arrested for drugs
353	Killed by guns
942	Hurt by guns
8,480	Arrested for violent crimes
40,279	Have babies

List the problems in order from the most common to the least common. The first one is done for you.

1. <u>Hurt in car accidents involving alcohol</u>

2. _____

3. _____

4. _____

5. _____

6. _____

7. _____

Read this information about the Urban Angels.

URBAN ANGELS

A program to address important issues facing American teenagers

Curtis Sliwa speaks to Urban Angels at their two-year anniversary

Curtis Sliwa, "Rocky Pasta e fagioli," Mary "Gold Card" Galda, and Curtis's mother, Frances Sliwa

Guardian Angel K.C. and her daughter, Urban Angel Rosie

Urban Angels at a graffiti paint-out

Frequently Asked Questions about the Urban Angels Life Skills Program

1 **What is the Urban Angels Life Skills Program?**

Urban Angels is a group for teenagers. The Guardian Angels started Urban Angels to support at-risk teens in the South Bronx in New York City. The Urban Angels Life Skills Program helps teens avoid drugs, gangs, guns, crime, and other trouble. The program wants teens to stay in school and to become positive members of their community.

2 **What do Urban Angels do?**

Urban Angels do many things. They have activities after school two days a week and two Saturdays a month. These activities are educational and fun.

3 Urban Angels go on trips to museums in New York City and to other places outside the city. They visit businesses to learn about different jobs. Most important, Urban Angels help out in their community. For

example, Urban Angels paint over graffiti at neighborhood "paint-outs." At "park clean-ups" they go to city parks and make them beautiful again.

4 **What do Urban Angels learn?**

Urban Angels take special classes. In class, they learn about social issues. They also learn how to stop problems in their community. They learn to take care of themselves, their families, and their neighbors. These teenagers become role models for younger kids. Most important, Urban Angels learn to respect themselves. They learn that they are important members of their community.

5 **Why do Urban Angels have nicknames?**

Urban Angels have nicknames to show their personalities and their goals for the future. For example, one young man has the nickname "Bear." He likes his nickname because he is big like a bear. He also likes this nickname because bears are strong, but they take care of their families, too.

6 **Can I become an Urban Angel?**

Today, you can become an Urban Angel if you are a teenager from the South Bronx. In the future, there might be Urban Angel groups in other cities.

7 **Who pays for the Urban Angels program?**

The New York City government and generous people from New York City support the Urban Angels program.

8 **How can I help?**

For more information and to learn how you can support the Urban Angels, write to us at:

The Alliance of the Guardian Angels
982 East 89th Street
Brooklyn, New York 11236 USA

B. READING FOR MAIN IDEAS

*Check (✓) the **true** sentences.*

The Urban Angels program:

_____   1. is for adults.

_____   2. helps its members feel good about themselves.

_____   3. finds jobs for its members.

_____   4. teaches its members about social issues.

_____   5. teaches young people about community service.

C. READING FOR DETAILS

Complete the sentences. Match the words on the left with the words on the right.

<u>c</u>   1. The Guardian Angels . . .

_____   2. The South Bronx . . .

_____   3. The Urban Angels program . . .

_____   4. Their nicknames . . .

_____   5. On weekends and after school, Urban Angels . . .

_____   6. Teens under 18 years of age who live in the South Bronx . . .

_____   7. The money for the program . . .

_____   8. If you want to help the Urban Angels, . . .

a. comes from the City of New York and from generous people.

b. go on "paint-outs" and "park clean-ups."

c. started the Urban Angels program.

d. is a neighborhood in New York City.

e. you can write to the Guardian Angels for more information.

f. helps teens stay away from trouble.

g. can become Urban Angels.

h. show their personalities and goals.

D. READING BETWEEN THE LINES

Look at Reading One again. Answer the following question. Check (✓) all the best answers. Then discuss your ideas with a partner.

Why do teenagers join the Urban Angels program?

Teenagers join the Urban Angels program to _____.

_____   1. become a member of a group

_____   2. meet friends

_____   3. learn how to paint

_____   4. get a nickname

_____   5. find a job

_____   6. leave the South Bronx

_____   7. avoid crime

_____   8. make their parents happy

_____   9. help the South Bronx

_____   10. your idea: _____

READING TWO: Two Real Angels

A. EXPANDING THE TOPIC

Read about Kathy and Melissa.

Two Real Angels

Kathy Santiago and Melissa Carrero are Urban Angels.
Today they became Junior Associates—leaders of the younger
Urban Angels.

"I learned to respect myself. I know if I need to do
something, I can do it. I want to be a fashion designer. I
feel I can reach my goals. I like Urban Angels because I like
helping and teaching others."

—Kathy "Classy" Santiago, age 15

"I learned that I can do anything. In the future, I want to
be an actress. I like being an Urban Angel because I can
teach people what I have learned."

—Melissa "Crazy Legs" Carrero, age 15

Urban Angels Kathy Santiago and Melissa
Carrero

Read each sentence. Circle the answer that completes the sentence.

1. The Urban Angels help Kathy and Melissa to _____.

   a. get a job
   b. have confidence

2. In the future, Melissa wants to be _____.

   a. a fashion designer
   b. an actress

3. Both Kathy and Melissa _____.

   a. like teaching people
   b. want to be Guardian Angels

B. LINKING READINGS ONE AND TWO

Look at Readings One and Two again. Then imagine that you are Melissa or Kathy. Write a letter to a friend. Tell your friend about your experience as an Urban Angel.

_____
(Today's date)

Dear _____,
(Your friend's name)

Hi. How are you doing? I'm fine, but I miss you.

This year I joined the Urban Angels. I'm really excited about it.

After school and on weekends, Urban Angels _____

_____

_____. For example, we _____

_____.

_____.

I like being an Urban Angel because _____

_____. I am learning to _____

_____.

If you move back to New York, I hope you will join the Urban

Angels, too.

I hope you are having fun in school this year. Write back soon.

Best regards,

_____
(Your name)

5 REVIEWING LANGUAGE

A. EXPLORING LANGUAGE

Work with a partner. Look at the word pairs. The two words in each pair are related in the same way. Complete the word pairs with a word from the list below.

~~avoid~~   generous   respect
crime   nickname   support
dangerous   positive   teenager

Example

afraid : scared   stay away from : avoid

Afraid and *scared* are synonyms. They have similar meanings. *Stay away from* and *avoid* are also synonyms.

1. start : begin   help : _____

2. strength : strong   danger : _____

3. lazy : energetic   negative : _____

4. ad : advertisement   teen: _____

5. dislike : like   disrespect : _____

6. Robert : Bob   name : _____

7. takes : greedy   gives : _____

8. team : baseball   gang : _____

B. WORKING WITH WORDS

Complete the paragraphs on page 59 with words from the list. Use each word only once.

at-risk   members   support
avoid   positive   teach
crime   role models   ~~teenagers~~

DISCIPLINE, ACTION, RESPONSIBILITY IN EDUCATION

DAREarts is a special program for kids 9 to 14 years old, not just for

_____teenagers_____. These kids study music, dance, theater, fashion,
1.

literature, and art history. DAREarts wants _____ kids to
2.

learn about the arts and to _____ drugs, gangs, and
3.

_____.
4.

The DAREarts teachers (called "mentors") are famous artists. These

artists are _____ for the DAREarts students. DAREarts
5.

students work with their teachers. Then, they return to their schools and

_____ their classmates about art.
6.

DAREarts helps young people feel good about themselves. These kids

become active _____ of their school community. As a
7.

result, they do better in school, and they learn to see their future in a

more _____ way.
8.

For more information about how you can _____
9.

DAREarts, write to us at:

DAREarts Foundation, Inc.
18444 Centreville Creek Road
Caledon East, Ontario, Canada
L0N1E0
1-888-540-arts

SKILLS FOR EXPRESSION

A. GRAMMAR: Pronouns and Possessive Adjectives

1 *Read this paragraph. Look at the underlined words. Draw an arrow from each underlined word to the noun it refers to. Then answer the questions.*

What Do Urban Angels Do?

Urban Angels have many activities after school and on Saturdays. They go on trips to local museums and to other places outside the city. They also visit businesses to learn about different jobs. Most important, Urban Angels help out in their community. For example, Urban Angels paint over graffiti at neighborhood "paint-outs." At "park clean-ups" they go to city parks and make them beautiful again.

1. Which underlined word is a subject?

2. Which underlined word is an object?

3. Which underlined word shows possession?

FOCUS ON GRAMMAR

See pronouns and possessive adjectives in *Focus on Grammar,* Introductory.

Pronouns and Possessive Adjectives

A *pronoun* is a word that takes the place of a noun. Pronouns are useful when you don't want to repeat a noun in a sentence.

1. *Subject pronouns* take the place of the subject in a sentence. Subject pronouns include *I, you, he, she, it, we,* and *they.*	**Subject** **Urban Angels** have many activities. **Subject pronoun** **They** go on trips to local museums. **You** can become an Urban Angel.

2. *Object pronouns* take the place of an object. Objects usually come after the verb. Object pronouns also come after prepositions like *for, to,* and *from.*

Object pronouns include *me, you, him, her, it, us,* and *them.*

Urban Angels like to help
Object
people.
Object pronoun
Urban Angels teach **them** about safety.

The Urban Angels program needs support. The New York City government helps pay for **it**.

3. *Possessive adjectives* are like pronouns. They show possession or ownership. They always come before a noun.

Possessive adjectives include *my, your, his, her, its, our,* and *their.*

Urban Angels help out in **their** community.

My goal is to be a fashion designer.

Kelly isn't an Urban Angel, but **her** friend is.

2 *Read these sentences about Curtis Sliwa. Complete each sentence with **he, him,** or **his.***

1. Curtis Sliwa started a recycling program when ___he___ was only 14 years old.

2. _____ used the money from recycling to help children in _____ neighborhood.

3. When _____ was 15 years old, _____ saved a family from a fire in their house.

4. The *New York Daily News* named _____ "Boy of the Year."

5. When _____ was 16 years old, _____ went to the White House.

6. President Nixon gave _____ an award for _____ community service.

7. After high school, _____ worked at a McDonald's restaurant in the South Bronx.

8. _____ started a community clean-up program.

9. Other McDonald's employees helped _____.

10. _____ started the Guardian Angels in 1979.

11. When _____ was young, _____ parents taught _____ to take care of _____ community.

12. _____ is still taking care of his community today.

3 *Wanda "Lipstick" Ayala is a Guardian Angel. Read these paragraphs about Wanda. Complete the sentences with **she, her, he, they,** or **them.***

Wanda "Lipstick" Ayala

Wanda "Lipstick" Ayala is 35 years old. __She__ lives in
                                          1.

Washington, D.C., with _____ three children and _____
                          2.   3.

husband. _____ works for the United States Postal Service.
            4.

_____ also helps out in _____ community.
   5.   6.

Lipstick and _____ little brother grew up in a dangerous
                7.

neighborhood in Washington, D.C. _____ loved each other very
                                    8.

much. For many years, Wanda tried to protect _____ brother from
                                                9.

drugs. Unfortunately, _____ had a drug problem, and _____
                            10.   11.

died in 1996.

  After _____ brother died, Lipstick became a Guardian Angel.
                12.

_____ nickname is "Lipstick" because _____ always wears
      13.   14.

bright red lipstick.

  In _____ free time, _____ helps young children and teenagers.
        15.   16.

Wanda says, "All children are important. People have to take care of

_____."
      17.

B. STYLE: Writing a Personal Letter

1 *A personal letter has five parts: a date, greeting, message, closing, and signature. Read your personal letter on page 57. Then label the five parts.*

Writing a Personal Letter

People write personal letters to their friends and family members. Here are the five parts of a personal letter.

1. **Date:** Write the date in the in the top right corner.

2. **Greeting:** Begin with "Dear" and the person's name.

3. **Message:** Write your message in paragraphs.

4. **Closing:** End your letter with "Sincerely," "Best wishes," "Best regards," "Love," or something similar.

5. **Signature:** Write your name after the closing.

Use these five parts when you write a letter to your friends and family.

2 *Imagine that you have a friend or family member in another city or town. Complete this personal letter. Tell your friend or family member about teenagers in your city or town. Try to use pronouns and possessive adjectives when you can.*

_____

_____,

    In English class, we are learning about teens in the South Bronx. Let me tell you about teenagers in my community.

    Most teens here are _____

_____.

    Some teens have problems, such as _____

_____. They _____

_____

_____.

    Other teens _____

_____.

    I hope _____

_____.

                      _____,

                       _____

Label the five parts of your letter.

ON YOUR OWN

A. WRITING TOPICS

Choose one of the following writing topics. Use some of the vocabulary, grammar, and style from this unit.

1. What is one way people are trying to help at-risk young people in your school or community? Write a paragraph. First describe the problem. Then write about how people are trying to help.

2. Guardian Angels and Urban Angels have nicknames. Their nicknames say something about their personalities and their goals.

   Do you have a nickname now? Did you have one in the past? What is it? Do you like it? How did you get this nickname? Write a paragraph about your nickname.

   If you don't have a nickname, choose a nickname for yourself. Then explain how this nickname fits your personality and your goals for the future. Write a paragraph about this nickname.

3. Imagine you work for the Guardian Angels in your city or town. Design and write an advertisement for the Urban Angels. Use words and pictures to get young people to join the Urban Angels program in your community.

B. FIELDWORK

Where can teenagers in your community go for help? Find one organization that helps teenagers in your city or town. Collect information and pictures, if possible, about this organization.

1. Fill in the information below.

Organization: _____

Address: _____
                    Street   City

Telephone: _____

E-mail or Web address (if available): _____

2. Check (✓) all correct answers.

What kind of organization is it? Is it:

_____ a government organization?

_____ a religious organization?

_____ an independent organization?

_____ other: _____

What problems do the teens have? Do they have:

_____ family problems?

_____ school problems?

_____ problems with other teens?

_____ other: _____

How do they help? Do they give people:

_____ money?

_____ a job?

_____ a place to live?

_____ advice?

_____ clothes?

_____ food?

_____ other: _____

3. Write a short paragraph about the organization.

4. Share your writing and pictures with a partner. Read your partner's paragraph. Then answer the questions.
   a. What is the writer's main idea?
   b. Is the main idea of the paragraph in the first sentence?
   c. Is there one sentence you do not understand? Underline it. Ask your partner to explain it to you.

GOING OUT OF BUSINESS

1 APPROACHING THE TOPIC

A. PREDICTING

Look at the picture. Discuss these questions with the class.

1. Is Colin's Coffee Shop open or closed? How do you know?
2. What does "out of business" mean?
3. Do you know of a store in your city or community that went out of business?

B. SHARING INFORMATION

Chain stores are usually owned by large companies. A chain has many stores with the same name. For example, Starbucks is a coffee bar chain. You can see Starbucks coffee bars in many different cities. *Locally owned businesses* (also called *family-owned businesses*) are usually small and owned by people in the community.

1 *Work in a small group. Make a list of the stores in your city or community. Put them in two groups: **locally owned** or **chain**.*

LOCALLY OWNED	CHAIN

2 *Do you go to the stores listed in Exercise 1? Talk with your group about why or why not. Look at the possible reasons and think of your own reasons.*

Positive Reasons

It has more products.
It has better products.
It has better service.
It is near my home.

Negative Reasons

It doesn't have the things I want.
I don't like the products.
The service isn't good.
It's too far away from my home.

Your own reasons: _____

2 PREPARING TO READ

A. BACKGROUND

With a partner, read this ad for Stamford, Connecticut. It gives all the reasons people and businesses should move to Stamford. Then answer the questions below.

Welcome to Stamford, CT
"The City That Works"

- Beautiful homes
- Friendly neighbors
- Hotels
- Parks and gardens
- Great public schools
- Public golf courses
- Family-owned businesses
- The University of Connecticut at Stamford
- Beaches
- Large corporations
- 50 minutes north of New York City
- Theaters
- Restaurants

Move your family or business to Stamford today!

---

1. Why is Stamford a good place for families?

2. Why is Stamford a good place for businesses?

3. Is your city or town a good place for families? For businesses? Why or why not? Share your ideas with the class.

B. VOCABULARY FOR COMPREHENSION

1 *Match the phrases on the left with the places on the right.*

  __d__   1. Buy books or magazines   **a.** electronics store

_____ 2. Get a haircut   **b.** video store

_____ 3. Get some medicine or aspirin   **c.** barbershop

_____ 4. Rent a movie   **d.** bookstore

_____ 5. Buy pens, pencils, or paper   **e.** hardware store

_____ 6. Buy a TV, CD player, or VCR   **f.** office supply store

_____ 7. Buy materials and tools to build   **g.** drugstore
            or fix things in your home

2 *Write sentences using the words and phrases above. Follow the example.*

1. I can buy books or magazines at a bookstore. _____

2. _____

3. _____

4. _____

5. _____

6. _____

7. _____

3 *Read the sentences. Then write each underlined word next to the correct definition in the list that follows on page 71.*

1. There are two fast-food restaurants nearby. The two restaurants <u>compete</u> for customers.

2. One <u>benefit</u> of living in a big city is good public transportation.

3. These shirts usually cost $25. Today they are only $20. What a great <u>discount</u>!

4. I'm not the boss. I'm an <u>employee</u>.

5. The prices at that clothing store <u>increase</u> every year. Clothing is getting very expensive.

6. My mother always shops at Shaw's supermarket. She is a <u>loyal</u> customer.

7. I like large stores because they have a better <u>selection</u>. I can find everything I need.

8. This is my barbershop. I am the <u>owner</u>.

9. At Christmas time, Borders Books has a lot of <u>customers</u>. They buy books to give as Christmas presents.

_____ a. a good thing; something that is helpful to you

_____ b. a lower price than usual

_____ c. a person who has or owns something

_____ d. not changing; faithful

_____ e. people who buy things from a store or company

_____ f. to become more in price or number

_____ g. to try to be the best at something

_____ h. someone who works in a store or for a company

_____ i. choice

3 READING ONE: The Death of the Family-Owned Video Store?

A. INTRODUCING THE TOPIC

Richard Woodroof is the owner of Captain Video. Captain Video is a family-owned video store in Stamford, Connecticut. Two big chain video stores are now open in Stamford. Mr. Woodroof sends a newsletter to all his customers. The newsletter is called "The Captain's Call."

Work with a partner. Before you read, think about "The Captain's Call." Check (✓) the words you think you will see in this newsletter.

_____ expert   _____ online   _____ service

_____ gallery   _____ rare   _____ support

_____ goal   _____ self-esteem   _____ volunteer

Summer Edition

Volume 2.2

The Captain's Call

1034 High Ridge Road

Stamford, CT

The Death of the Family-Owned Video Store?

1   Large chain stores are killing family-owned businesses in Stamford. First, Borders Books, a large chain store, opened and a small bookstore went out of business. Then Genovese, a large drugstore chain, opened and a small drugstore went out of business. Small stores can't compete with these large chain stores.

2   Other family-owned businesses in Stamford are in danger: a hardware store, a barbershop, an office supply store, an electronics store, and a video store. Captain Video! If you don't do something now, your life in Stamford will change forever.

3   Today, two big video chain stores—Blockbuster Video, and Tower Record and Video—are open in Stamford, and our store, Captain Video, is in danger.

4   Captain Video can stay in business only if you help. You, our loyal customers, know the benefits of being Captain Video customers. The benefits are:

5   Selection—We have more movies than other video stores in Stamford. We have 15,000 tapes, digital video discs (DVDs), and video games. We are always adding more.

6   Service—The employees at Captain Video love movies and know a lot about them, so we can give personal service to all our customers.

7   Prices—Because of competition with Blockbuster, we had to increase our prices a little. But we still have great discounts. For example, if you rent more than one video, you pay less. We also have longer rental times on most videos, DVDs, and games.

8   Thank you for being loyal customers. Please continue to support Captain Video and other family-owned businesses. With your support, we can stay open.

9   Life in Stamford will change forever if we lose our family-owned businesses. Only YOU can stop the chain stores from changing Stamford!

B. READING FOR MAIN IDEAS

Read each pair of sentences. Check (✓) the one sentence in each pair that is true.

1. ____ **a.** Blockbuster Video is in danger of going out of business.

   _✓_ **b.** Captain Video is in danger of going out of business.

2. ____ **a.** Small, locally owned stores are closing in Stamford.

   ____ **b.** Large chain stores are closing in Stamford.

3. ____ **a.** Mr. Woodroof wants the customers to support the chain stores.

   ____ **b.** Mr. Woodroof wants the customers to support the smaller stores.

4. ____ **a.** Mr. Woodroof is afraid that life in his town is changing.

   ____ **b.** Mr. Woodroof is happy that life in his town is changing.

5. ____ **a.** Mr. Woodroof's customers are loyal to Blockbuster Video.

   ____ **b.** Mr. Woodroof's customers are loyal to Captain Video.

C. READING FOR DETAILS

Read each sentence. Circle the answer that completes the sentence.

1. Borders is the name of a large _____ chain.

   a. (bookstore)   **c.** electronics store
   b. drugstore   **d.** video store

2. Captain Video is trying to compete with _____.

   a. Blockbuster   **c.** Genovese
   b. Borders Books   **d.** Starbucks

3. Captain Video has more _____ than other video stores in Stamford.

   a. customers   c. movies
   b. employees   d. video games

4. Captain Video customers are _____.

   a. changing   c. loyal
   b. friendly   d. personal

5. Captain Video employees know a lot about _____.

   a. chain stores   c. video games
   b. customers   d. movies

6. Captain Video recently increased its _____.

   a. prices   c. employees
   b. videos   d. customers

7. Captain Video has special _____ on video rentals.

   a. selections   c. customers
   b. discounts   d. service

D. READING BETWEEN THE LINES

*Work with a partner. Read each sentence. What do you think? Why is Richard Woodroof upset? Write **T** (true) or **F** (false). Then discuss your answers with the class.*

_____   1. He doesn't want life in Stamford to change.

_____   2. He doesn't want his personal life to change.

_____   3. He doesn't like competition.

_____   4. He might lose his business.

_____   5. He is worried about his customers.

_____   6. He thinks all chain stores are bad.

READING TWO: Did You Know?

A. EXPANDING THE TOPIC

Read this information about Blockbuster Video.

Our goal is to be the world's best home entertainment store. We want to offer our customers great service, selection, and value. We want to build a strong relationship with our customers and offer them new and better products and services.

Did you know?

In the United States . . .

◆ BLOCKBUSTER has more than 5,700 video stores and 78,000 employees.

◆ There is a BLOCKBUSTER store in most neighborhoods.

◆ Each BLOCKBUSTER store has about 10,000 to 14,000 videos.

◆ There are more than 38 million BLOCKBUSTER customers in the United States.

◆ More than 2 million customers visit a BLOCKBUSTER store every day.

◆ Customers rent about 1,500 videos from BLOCKBUSTER stores in the United States each minute.

Internationally . . .

◆ There are more than 2,000 BLOCKBUSTER stores in 26 countries in Europe, Asia, South America, and Canada.

◆ There are more than 15,000 BLOCKBUSTER employees in international stores.

◆ The country with the most BLOCKBUSTER stores is the United Kingdom, with more than 700.

◆ The country with the fewest BLOCKBUSTER stores is Uruguay, with two.

◆ The newest BLOCKBUSTER store is in Costa Rica.

Blockbuster uses numbers to show us how big it is. Fill in the blanks with the correct numbers.

1. Blockbuster has more than _____2 million_____ customers every day.

2. It has _____78,000_____ employees in the United States and more than _____ employees in international stores.

3. There are Blockbuster stores in _____ countries in Europe, Asia, South America, and Canada.

4. There are more than _____ Blockbuster video stores in the United States and more than _____ internationally.

5. Uruguay has only _____ Blockbuster store so far.

6. Blockbuster has more than _____ customers in the United States.

7. Each store has between _____ and _____ videos.

8. The United Kingdom has more than _____ Blockbuster stores.

9. Every minute, customers in the United States rent about _____ videos from Blockbuster.

B. LINKING READINGS ONE AND TWO

*Work with a partner. Look at Readings One and Two again. Decide who said each statement: the owner of Captain Video (**CV**), Blockbuster Video (**BB**), or both (**B**). Write your answers. Then share them with the class. More than one answer is possible.*

_____ 1. Chain stores hurt the community.

_____ 2. Competition is good for businesses.

_____ 3. We care about our customers.

_____ 4. We have more videos to rent.

_____ 5. Our company creates more jobs.

_____ 6. We give our customers personal service.

_____ 7. Our prices are lower.

_____ 8. We have more stores.

_____ 9. We love movies.

5 REVIEWING LANGUAGE

A. EXPLORING LANGUAGE

Look at this chart. It shows some important word forms. (It does not give all the possible word forms.) Then complete the sentences below.

VERB	NOUN	ADJECTIVE
compete	competition, competitor	***
employ	employee	***
increase (in **crease**)	increase (**in** crease)	***
***	loyalty	loyal
serve	service	***
own	owner	***

compete, competition, competitors

1. McDonald's and Wendy's are ___competitors___. They are both fast-food restaurants.

2. McDonald's and Wendy's _____ for more customers.

3. The _____ between McDonald's and Wendy's is very strong.

employees, employs

4. Blockbuster Video _____ over 93,000 people around the word.

5. In the United States, Blockbuster Video has 78,000 _____.

loyal, loyalty

6. Our _____ customers always come to our store.

7. We need your _____ to stay in business.

increase (verb), **increase** (noun)

8. Captain Video didn't want to _____ its prices too much.

9. The _____ wasn't very big. It was only about 50 cents.

serves, service

10. Starbucks _____ very good coffee.

11. The _____ at Starbucks is usually very good, too.

owner, owns

12. My brother _____ three hardware stores.

13. He is the _____ of three hardware stores.

B. WORKING WITH WORDS

Read the review of the movie You've Got Mail *on page 79. Fill in the blanks with one of the words from the list. Use each word only one time.*

~~bookstore~~
business
chain
competitors
customers
discounts
loyal
owner
selection
service

Movie Review

You've Got Mail is a romantic comedy about two bookstore owners. Kathleen Kelly (Meg Ryan) is the owner of a children's ___bookstore___. Her mother
1.
started this small bookstore when Kelly was a little girl.

Joe Fox (Tom Hanks) is the

_____ of Fox Books, a large
2.

bookstore _____ in New
3.

York. Fox and Kelly are

_____.
4.

Some of Kelly's _____ customers start to shop at Fox Books. Fox
5.

Books has a large _____ of books. It also offers big
6.

_____ on its books. But Fox's employees do not know a lot about
7.

children's books.

Kelly knows a lot about children's books. She also offers her _____
8.

a lot of personal _____.
9.

Will Kelly's family-owned store go out of _____ or will it stay open?
10.

Will Fox and Kelly live happily ever after? Watch *You've Got Mail* and find out.

6. SKILLS FOR EXPRESSION

A. GRAMMAR: *There is/There are*

Young-Hee and Sofia are friends. Young-Hee is from Korea, and Sofia is from Australia. They spent four years at the same university in the United States. Young-Hee returned home to Korea, and Sofia went back to Australia. Then Young-Hee wrote a letter to her.

1 *Read Young-Hee's letter. Then answer the questions. Discuss your answers with a partner.*

May 15th

Dear Sofia,

How are you? I miss you, and I miss school. But I am happy to be back in Seoul, too.

Seoul is different now. I am really upset about one change. Soon they are going to put a McDonald's restaurant on my beautiful street! I can't believe it!

My neighborhood is near Yonsei University in Seoul. It is very quiet here. There are a lot of students and professors in my neighborhood. There are also many family-owned businesses on the main street. There is a flower shop. Also, there are two video stores, a bakery, a vegetable shop, and a clothing store. But there aren't any large chain stores, and there isn't a McDonald's. Not yet! I don't want my neighborhood to change.

I hope you are OK. Can you visit Korea soon? We can go to McDonald's together. Just kidding.

Love,

Young-Hee

1. How many times does Young-Hee use *there is*, *there isn't*, *there are*, and *there aren't*? Underline them.

2. What nouns follow *there is* and *there isn't*? Make a list.

3. What nouns follow *there are* and *there aren't*? Make a list.

There is/There are

FOCUS ON GRAMMAR

See *there is* and *there are* in *Focus on Grammar*, Introductory.

1. Use *there is* or *there are* to describe something in the present.	
There is/are + noun	**There is a bakery** on my street.
There is + singular count noun	**There is a bank** on Main Street.
There are + plural count noun	**There are a lot of students** in my neighborhood.
There is + non-count noun	**There is a lot of traffic** in Seoul.
2. Use *there was* or *there were* to describe something in the past.	**There was** a flower shop on my street. **There were** a lot of people on my street.
3. Use the contractions *isn't/aren't* and *wasn't/weren't* with *there* in the negative.	**There isn't** a McDonald's nearby.
4. For questions, put *there* after *is/are* and *was/were*. Use *any* with *yes/no* questions about plural nouns and non-count nouns.	**Is there** a movie theater nearby? **Were there any restaurants** in your neighborhood? **Is there any traffic** in your neighborhood at night?
5. Do not confuse *there is* and *there are* with *there. There* means "in that location."	Seoul is a beautiful city. There are some beautiful parks **there** *(in Seoul).*

2 *Read Sofia's reply to Young-Hee, shown on page 82. Then choose the correct verbs to complete her sentences.*

June 25th

Dear Young-Hee,

Thanks for your letter. I miss you, too. But I don't miss school! There

_____ a lot of changes here in Perth, too. I'm really surprised!
　　1. is/are

My street is quiet, but there _____ two busy streets nearby,
　　　　　　　　　　　　　　2. is/are

Main Street and Queens Road. There _____ a lot of cars on these
　　　　　　　　　　　　　　　　　3. is/are

streets. When I was young, there _____ much noise, but today
　　　　　　　　　　　　　　4. wasn't/weren't

there _____ more people and cars.
　　5. is/are

Here's another change. There _____ two Starbucks coffee bars
　　　　　　　　　　　　　　6. is/are

near my apartment! Two! Five years ago there _____ only one
　　　　　　　　　　　　　　　　　　7. was/were

small café. I ate breakfast there every morning. But it's gone! There

_____ a hardware store there now.
　　8. is/are

Luckily, one thing did not change. There _____ still a beautiful
　　　　　　　　　　　　　　　　　9. is/are

old movie theater on the corner of Main Street and Queens Road. It's

called the Astor Theater. It is one of my favorite places.

_____ there any chance you can visit me in Australia?
　　10. Is/Are

I hope to visit you in Korea soon. By the way, I love McDonald's!

Love, Sofia

3 *Work with a partner. Write five questions about your partner's neighborhood or city. Use* Is/Are there *and* Was/Were there. *Then exchange books and answer each other's questions. Use* There is/are, *and* There was/were.

1. <u>Are there any fast-food restaurants nearby?</u>

2. _____

3. _____

4. _____

5. _____

6. _____

1. <u>Yes, there is. There is a McDonald's.</u>

2. _____

3. _____

4. _____

5. _____

6. _____

B. STYLE: Describing a Place Using Spatial Order

1 *Read this paragraph about High Ridge Road in Stamford, Connecticut. As you read, continue drawing the arrow (→) from place to place. Then compare your arrows with your classmates'.*

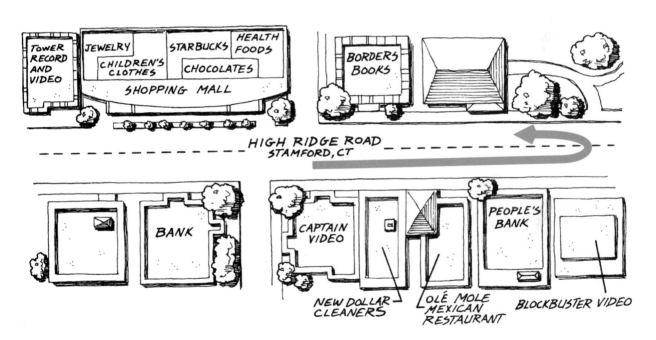

Captain Video is on High Ridge Road in Stamford, Connecticut. There are a lot of family-owned businesses and chain stores near Captain Video. Blockbuster Video is four doors away on the right. Borders Books is across the street from Captain Video. There is a small shopping mall across from Borders. In the shopping mall there is a health food store, a chocolate store, a Starbucks coffee bar, a children's clothing store, and a jewelry store. Tower Record and Video is to the left of the shopping mall.

Describing a Place Using Spatial Order

Spatial[1] *order* means organizing ideas by location or place. For example, you can go from left to right, up or down, or around or across.

Use prepositions to show location:

across (from)	in front of	on the right
around the corner (from)	next to	to the left (of)
behind	on	to the right (of)
between	on the left	

When you describe a place with spatial order, your reader will understand you more easily.

2 *Write a short paragraph that describes one of the following places. Use spatial order and* there is/there are.

1. part of a street in your neighborhood or city

2. your classroom

3. your bedroom

4. your favorite room in your home

ON YOUR OWN

A. WRITING TOPICS

Choose one of the following writing topics. Use some of the vocabulary, grammar, and style from this unit.

1. Write about your neighborhood or city. Are there any changes? Do things look different from five or ten years ago? Write a short paragraph. Use spatial order.

---

[1]*spatial:* pronounced **spashəl**

2. Is your city or town a good place to live? Is it a good place for businesses? Explain your answer in two paragraphs. Write one paragraph for each question.

3. In many places, large businesses are becoming more popular. Small, family-owned businesses are going out of business. Is this a good change? Write your answer in one paragraph.

B. FIELDWORK

Interview the owner or an employee of a family-owned business.

1. Write down the answers to these questions. Think of your own questions, too.

   a. What is the name of the business?

   _____

   b. What kind of business is it?

   _____

   c. Is it a small business or a large business?

   _____

   d. What year did you open your business?

   _____

   e. Has your business changed since it opened? How?

   _____

   f. Is there any competition with other businesses? Which ones?

   _____

   g. Do you like working here? Why or why not?

   _____

   h. Your questions: _____

   _____

2. Write one paragraph about this business. Use the information you collected.

3. Share your paragraph with a partner. Read your partner's paragraph. Then answer these questions.

    a. Did the writer indent the first line of the paragraph?

    b. Did the writer use margins correctly?

    c. Do you have one question about the business that the writer did not include in the paragraph? Write it here.

_____

FLYING HIGH AND LOW

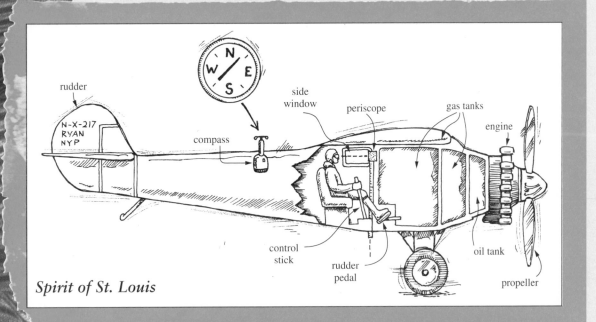

Spirit of St. Louis

1 APPROACHING THE TOPIC

A. PREDICTING

Look at the picture. Discuss these questions with the class.

1. What is the *Spirit of St. Louis*?
2. Does it look old or new?
3. Do you want to take a long trip in this airplane today? Why or why not?

B. SHARING INFORMATION

1 *Famous people have high points (good times) and low points (bad times) in their lives. Work with a partner. Look at the list of names below. Write the correct name next to the high point and low point in that person's life. Compare your answers with the class.*

Christopher Reeve   Pu Yi
Nelson Mandela   Marilyn Monroe
Vincent van Gogh   Richard Nixon
Diana Spencer

Name	High Point	Low Point
1. _____	He was the president of the United States.	He quit his job in 1974.
2. _____	She was a Hollywood movie star in the 1950s and 1960s.	Her real name was Norma Jean Baker. She was poor and unhappy as a child.
3. _____	He became the president of South Africa in 1994.	He was in jail for about 27 years.
4. _____	He was Superman in movies.	He had a serious horseback riding accident.
5. _____	He painted many beautiful works of art.	He cut off his ear.
6. _____	He was the emperor of China.	He lost his empire.
7. _____	She was a teacher, and she became a princess.	Her marriage to the Prince of Wales ended.

2 *Work with a partner. Interview each other. Ask: What was a good time in your life? What was a bad time? Then answer your partner's questions.*

2 PREPARING TO READ

A. BACKGROUND

Charles Lindbergh won a flying competition in his airplane, the Spirit of St. Louis. *Read this poster about the competition.*

Complete the sentences with the words below. Look at the poster again for help.

New York	Atlantic	Paris
$25,000	non-stop	~~Raymond Orteig~~

In 1919, __Raymond Orteig__ started a competition. He offered _____ to the first
                   1.   2.

pilot to fly _____ across the _____ Ocean between _____
               3.   4.   5.

and _____. In 1927, Charles Lindbergh was the winner.
      6.

B. VOCABULARY FOR COMPREHENSION

Read the words and their definitions. Then read about Lindbergh's trip on the Spirit of St. Louis *from San Diego to New York. Complete the sentences with words from the list.*

pilot: the person who flies an airplane

flight: a trip in an airplane

took off: left a place in an airplane; past form of *take off*

landed: arrived somewhere in an airplane

set a record: to do something faster or better than ever before

media: newspapers, magazines, radio, and television

contest: a game that people try to win; a competition

handsome: good-looking (usually for a man)

hero: someone you respect very much for doing something good

Flying to New York

In the 1920s flying airplanes was a new science. Charles Lindbergh, a ____handsome____
                                                                          1.

young airmail _____, was very interested in flying.
                    2.

On May 10, 1927, Lindbergh _____ from San Diego, California. He stopped
                                    3.

in St. Louis, Missouri, for gas and oil. Then he quickly continued on to New York to enter

Raymond Orteig's _____.
                          4.

He _____ in New York on May 12th. He flew from San Diego to New York
        5.

in less than 22 hours. He _____ for the fastest _____ across the
                                6.   7.

United States.

This was only the beginning of Lindbergh's historic trip. Lindbergh was on his way to becoming

an international _____. The _____ followed him from then on.
                        8.   9.

3

READING ONE: Lindbergh Did It!

A. INTRODUCING THE TOPIC

*A **fool** is a person who is crazy or not very intelligent. At first, people called Lindbergh "The Flying Fool." Why do you think they called him this? Check (✓) the answers you think are correct.*

_____ The weather was bad.

_____ Lindbergh was too young to fly.

_____ The plane was too small to cross the ocean.

_____ Lindbergh was not a good student in school.

_____ The trip was too long.

Your ideas: _____

Read this newspaper story about Lindbergh's historic trip from New York to Paris.

Lindbergh Did It!

Paris Express News—May 27, 1927

1   Paris, France—One week ago, Charles Augustus Lindbergh was just a handsome, 25-year-old airmail pilot from a small town in the United States. Today he is the most famous man in the world and the most important man in the history of flying.

2   Last week, Lindbergh flew solo from New York to France. He was the first person to fly non-stop across the Atlantic Ocean alone. He also set the record for the longest non-stop flight.

3   Lindbergh took off on his historic flight on May 20th at 7:52 A.M. People called him "The Flying Fool." On that day, other pilots in the contest waited in New York because the weather was bad. Lindbergh did not wait. He took five sandwiches, a bottle of water, a notebook, a pen, and a compass. He didn't even have a radio. All he heard was the sound of the wind and the noise from the engine of the plane. He was in the air all alone with his thoughts, his hopes, and his fears.

4   After 3,610 miles, 33 hours and 30 minutes, and no sleep, Lindbergh landed in Paris on May 21st. At that moment, his life changed forever.

There were 150,000 excited people waiting to greet him. The international media was also there. Photographers and newspaper reporters wanted to be the first to tell the story about Lindbergh. When he got out of his plane and saw all the excitement, he knew that his life would never be the same again.

5   When he began this dangerous flight, he was a quiet young man from a quiet town. This morning, "Lucky Lindy" left Paris as an international hero.

B. READING FOR MAIN IDEAS

Read each sentence. Circle the answer that completes the sentence.

1. In 1927, Lindbergh set the record for the _____ non-stop flight.

    a. first
    b. longest
    c. highest

2. He was the first to fly non-stop from _____.

    a. France to the United States
    b. the United States to France
    c. New York to San Diego

3. The people waiting in Paris were very_____.

    a. excited
    b. quiet
    c. confused

4. Because of his historic flight, Lindbergh became very _____.

    a. handsome
    b. lucky
    c. famous

C. READING FOR DETAILS

Answer each question on page 93 using one of the numbers from the box. Write your answers in complete sentences.

one	33½
five	7:52
the 20th	3,610
the 21st	150,000
~~25~~	

1. How old was Lindbergh when he flew across the Atlantic?

   <u>Lindbergh was 25 years old when he flew across the Atlantic.</u>

2. On what date did he take off from New York?

   _____

3. At what time in the morning did he take off from New York?

   _____

4. How many people were on Lindbergh's plane when he flew across
   the Atlantic?

   _____

5. How many miles was Lindbergh's flight?

   _____

6. For how many hours was he in the air?

   _____

7. How many sandwiches did he bring on his trip?

   _____

8. On what date did he land in Paris?

   _____

9. About how many people greeted him when he arrived in Paris?

   _____

D. READING BETWEEN THE LINES

*Read "Lindbergh Did It!" again, and answer the following question.
First, discuss your ideas in a small group. Then write at least two
reasons. Share your sentences with your group.*

Why did Lindbergh fly across the Atlantic?

1. _____

2. _____

READING TWO: Timeline of Lindbergh's Life

A. EXPANDING THE TOPIC

1 *After his historic flight, Lindbergh was very famous. The media followed him everywhere. Read this timeline of his life.*

CHARLES LINDBERGH'S LIFE

Dates	What happened?
May 21, 1927	"Lucky Lindy" landed in Paris at 10:21 P.M.
May 21–31, 1927	He was welcomed in Europe by presidents, kings, and queens.
June 11, 1927	He met the U.S. president in Washington, D.C.
June 13, 1927	He received $25,000 from Raymond Orteig.
July 20–Oct. 23, 1927; Dec. 1927	He flew to 82 U.S. cities in 48 states and Latin America on a "friendship tour" in the *Spirit of St. Louis.*
Jan. 28, 1928	*Time* magazine made him "Man of the Year."
May 27, 1929	Lindbergh married Anne Morrow.
March 2, 1932	Someone kidnapped[1] his first child, Charles Jr.
April 1935	Lindbergh invented an "artificial heart."
Dec. 21, 1935	He moved with his wife and their second son, Jon, to England to protect them from the media.
Late 1930s–early 1940s	He visited airplane factories in Nazi Germany and other countries. People also called him "anti-American" and "a Nazi."
1954	He won the Pulitzer Prize for *The Spirit of St. Louis,* a book about his flight.
Late 1960s–early 1970s	He became an environmentalist. He worked to protect nature and animals in Africa, Asia, and the United States.
Aug. 26, 1974	He died of cancer in Maui, Hawaii, at the age of 72.

---

[1] *kidnap* (v): to take someone away illegally and ask for money for returning him or her
a *kidnapper* (n): a person who kidnaps someone

Work with a partner. Charles Lindbergh was not a simple man. He had many different jobs and responsibilities. Look at Reading Two again. Then make a list of Lindbergh's jobs and responsibilities.

Examples

He was a pilot.
He was a husband.

2 *What kind of person was Lindbergh? With your partner, choose **one** word to describe Lindbergh. Talk about why. Then share your choice with the class.*

simple	loyal
controversial	independent
adventurous	Your idea: _____

B. LINKING READINGS ONE AND TWO

1 *Look at Readings One and Two again. What were the high points and low points in Lindbergh's life? Write your answers below. Then discuss your answers with the class.*

HIGH POINTS	LOW POINTS
He set flying records.	His first son was kidnapped.

5 REVIEWING LANGUAGE

A. EXPLORING LANGUAGE

A *synonym* is a word that has a similar meaning to another word.

The **price** of the *Spirit of St. Louis* was $10,580.
The **cost** of the *Spirit of St. Louis* was $10,580.

The plane was **built** in San Diego, California.
The plane was **constructed** in San Diego, California.

Read each sentence. Change the underlined word to a synonym from Reading One on page 91. Follow the example. If you need help, look at the paragraph number in parentheses ( ).

took off
1. Lindbergh ~~departed~~ from New York on May 20, 1927.   (3)

2. The *Spirit of St. Louis* <u>arrived</u> in France on May 21, 1927.   (4)

3. He flew across the Atlantic <u>alone</u>.   (2)

4. Lindbergh was a <u>good-looking</u> man.   (1)

5. Lindbergh won the <u>competition</u> that Orteig started in 1919.   (3)

6. The <u>press</u> gave Lindbergh a lot of attention in the newspapers and on the radio.   (4)

7. Lindbergh became <u>well known</u> all over the world.   (1)

8. His historic <u>trip</u> changed his life.   (2)

9. Amelia Earhart was another famous <u>flier</u>.   (1)

B. WORKING WITH WORDS

Read the story about Amelia Earhart on page 97. Choose the words that complete the sentences.

Amelia Earhart (1897–1937?) was an American _____pilot_____.
                                                    1. pilot/writer

She became interested in _____ while working in Canada
                              2. landing/flying

during World War I. She began flying in 1922.

In 1928, Earhart became the first woman to fly across the Atlantic Ocean. This _____
                                                            3. flight/contest
made her very _____. But
                    4. famous/dangerous
Earhart was not the pilot on this flight. She was only a passenger.

Then she became the first woman to fly _____ across
                                              5. famous/solo

the Atlantic in 1932. She _____ from Harbour Grace,
                                6. took off/landed

Newfoundland and _____ near Londonderry, Ireland.
                         7. took off/landed

In 1937, Earhart and her navigator, Fred Noonan, tried to fly around

the world. Their _____ disappeared near Howland Island
                        8. compass/plane

in the Pacific Ocean. Today no one knows exactly what happened to

Earhart and Noonan.

SKILLS FOR EXPRESSION

A. GRAMMAR: The Simple Past

1 *Read these paragraphs. Underline the verbs that tell about the past. Then answer the questions.*

On March 1, 1932, someone <u>kidnapped</u> Charles and Anne Lindbergh's baby. The kidnapper left a note in the baby's bedroom. In the note, the kidnapper asked for $50,000. Lindbergh paid the money. Unfortunately, on May 12, 1932, a man found the baby. The baby was dead.

In 1935, the police arrested Bruno Richard Hauptmann. Hauptmann said, "I didn't do it!" Many people did not believe him. Hauptmann died in the electric chair[1] on April 2, 1936.

Today, a few people believe that Hauptmann did not kidnap the Lindbergh baby.

1. Which past tense verbs are regular? Make a list.
   (*Hint:* They end in *-ed.*)

2. Which past tense verbs are irregular? Make a list.

3. How do you form the simple past in negative sentences?

---

[1] *electric chair:* a chair that uses electricity to kill people as punishment for a crime

The Simple Past

FOCUS ON GRAMMAR

See the simple past of regular and irregular verbs in *Focus on Grammar,* Introductory.

1. Use the simple past tense to talk about actions completed in the past.	People **called** Lindbergh "The Flying Fool."	

	Base Form	**Simple Past**
2. To form the simple past tense:		
◆ For regular verbs, add -*ed* to the base form.	land	land**ed**
	return	return**ed**
◆ If the base form ends in *e,* add only -*d.*	receive	receive**d**
	live	live**d**
◆ If the base verb ends in a consonant followed by the letter *y,* change the *y* to *i,* then add -*ed.*	marry	marr**ied**
	try	tr**ied**
◆ If the base form ends with consonant-vowel-consonant, double the last consonant, then add -*ed.*	kidnap	kidna**pped**
	stop	sto**pped**

	Base Form	**Simple Past**
3. Many verbs have irregular forms.	become	**became**
Note: The simple past tense of *be* is *was* or *were,* and of *have* is *had.*	do	**did**
	fly	**flew**
	go	**went**
	take	**took**
	think	**thought**

4. To make negative statements, use: *didn't (did not)* + the base form	Lindbergh **didn't have** a radio with him.

5. To ask *wh-* questions, use: *Wh-* word + *did* + subject + base form. Note: If you do not know the *subject* of the question, do not use *did.*	**When did Earhart disappear?** Subject **Who kidnapped** the Lindbergh's baby? **What happened** to Lindbergh's baby?

6. To ask *yes/no* questions, use: *Did* + subject + base form	**Did Lindbergh win** Orteig's contest?

2 *Complete the paragraphs with the simple past tense form of the verbs.*

Raymond Orteig _____started_____ the flying contest for two reasons. First, Orteig
                        1. start

_____ to build friendship between the United States and France. He also
   2. want

_____ people to become more interested in flying.
   3. want

Five planes _____ to cross the Atlantic during the 1920s, but no one
                    4. try

_____ successful. The flight _____ very dangerous. Six men
   5. be   **6. be**

_____ trying to win the contest. Finally, Lindbergh _____ it. After
   7. die   **8. do**

Lindbergh _____ in Paris, people _____ him a hero. Later, he
              9. arrive   **10. call**

_____ one of the most famous men in the world.
   11. become

As a boy, Lindbergh _____ very independent. As an adult, he _____.
                        12. be   **13. not/change**

He _____ strong opinions. Lindbergh _____ really anti-American. He
      14. have   **15. not/be**

_____ the United States to enter World War II. He _____ that Germany
   16. not/want   **17. think**

_____ too strong. Many people _____ with his opinions. At that time,
   18. be   **19. not/agree**

they _____ Lindbergh _____ a hero at all.
        20. not/think   **21. be**

3 *Write questions about Charles Lindbergh. Write three yes/no questions and three* wh- *questions. Then share your questions with the class.*

Example

<u>Did Charles and Anne Lindbergh have more than one child?</u>

1. _____

2. _____

3. _____

Example

Why did Lindbergh and his family move to England in 1935?

4. _____

5. _____

6. _____

B. STYLE: Time Order

1 *Look at the map. Then read the sentences. Put the sentences in time order. Put* **1** *next to the first event,* **2** *next to the second event, and so on.*

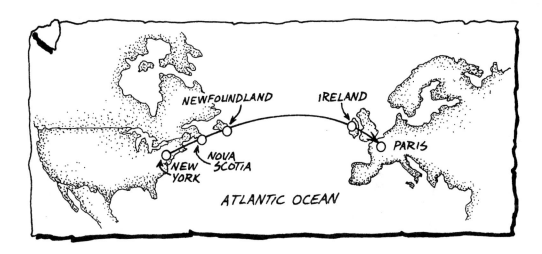

_____   **a.** People in Ireland saw his plane in the sky.

_____   **b.** He landed in Le Bourget Field near Paris at 10:24 P.M.

_____   **c.** He flew over the Eiffel Tower.

_____   **d.** Lindbergh flew over Nova Scotia and Newfoundland.

_____   **e.** Lindbergh traveled over the dark Atlantic Ocean toward Europe.

__1__   **f.** Lindbergh took off from Roosevelt Field in New York at 7:54 A.M.

_____   **g.** Thousands of people greeted him when he got out of the *Spirit of St. Louis.*

Time Order

When you tell a story, it is important to put the events in a clear order so your reader can understand easily. Use these words to help with time order:

Time Order Words

First,
Then,
Next,
Later,
Finally,

These time words usually come at the beginning of the sentence.

Lindbergh decided to enter Orteig's contest. **First,** he needed to build a lightweight airplane. **Then,** . . .

Use *finally* for the last sentence in your paragraph.

2 *Complete the paragraph with appropriate time order words. More than one answer is possible. Share your paragraph with a partner.*

Lindbergh planned his flight very carefully. _____, he took off from Roosevelt
                                                          1.
Field in New York at 7:54 A.M. and flew toward Nova Scotia and Newfoundland.

_____, Lindbergh traveled over the dark Atlantic Ocean toward Europe. People in
       2.
Ireland saw his plane in the sky. _____, he flew over the Eiffel Tower.
                                                3.

_____, he landed in Le Bourget Field near Paris at 10:24 P.M. When he got out of his
       4.
plane, thousands of people welcomed him to France.

3 *Look at Section 2B again on page 90. Rewrite "Flying to New York" using time order words.*

4 *Write one paragraph about a trip that you took. Use time order words and the simple past tense in your paragraph.*

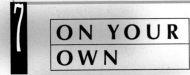

ON YOUR OWN

A. WRITING TOPICS

Choose one of the following writing topics. Use some of the vocabulary, grammar, and style from this unit.

1. Write a paragraph about a time when your life changed in a good way or in a bad way. What happened? How did you deal with the change? Use simple past verbs and time order.

2. Think about Charles Lindbergh's life. Then imagine that you are Charles Lindbergh. It is June 1974, and you are near the end of your life. Write a letter to your family. Tell them about some of the high points and low points of your life. Use simple past verbs and time order in your letter.

3. The artist Andy Warhol said that everyone has "15 minutes of fame." Write a paragraph about someone you know who became famous for a little while. What happened? Did the person change? Use simple past verbs and time order.

B. FIELDWORK

Think of a famous person who is not living today. Collect information about this person and pictures, if possible.

1. Look in the library and on the Internet for information about this person.

2. Make a timeline of this person's life like the timeline on page 94. Write the important dates in the "Dates" column. Then write a sentence about each date in the "What happened?" column. Include the good times and bad times in this person's life.

3. Write a paragraph about this person. Use simple past tense verbs when you write about past events. Also, use time order. Begin your paragraph with the sentence:

_____ had an interesting life.
    (name)

4. Share your writing with a partner. Read your partner's paragraph. Then answer these questions.

   a. Did the writer use simple past tense for past events?

   b. Did the writer use time order? Underline the time words.

   c. Is there one sentence you think is very interesting? Underline it. Tell your partner why you think it is interesting.

ARE WE THERE YET?

APPROACHING THE TOPIC

A. PREDICTING

Look at the picture. Discuss these questions with the class.

1. The woman is stuck in a traffic jam. Where is she going?
2. How is she feeling right now?

B. SHARING INFORMATION

Think of a time you were stuck in a traffic jam. Answer the questions. Then ask three classmates these questions. Write their answers below.

	YOU	STUDENT 1	STUDENT 2	STUDENT 3
Where were you? (What country? city? town?)				
Where were you going?				
Were you in a car? On a bus? Other?				
How long were you in traffic?				
What did you do in the car?				
How did you feel?				

2 PREPARING TO READ

A. BACKGROUND

A *trip* in a car is any time a person uses his or her car. A person can *take a trip* to the supermarket, to work, or on a vacation.

Look at the graph on page 107 about driving in the United States. Then answer the questions.

Increase in Driving in the United States in the 1990s

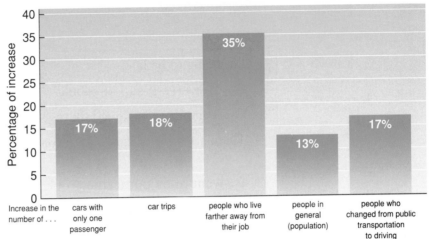

1. What does this graph show?
2. What is the biggest reason for the increase in driving?
3. Which was greater: the increase in car trips or population?
4. What percentage of people changed from public transportation to driving?

B. VOCABULARY FOR COMPREHENSION

1 *Look at the picture carefully. Then write words from the box on the numbered lines in the picture.*

commuter
helicopter
highway
lanes
subway
train
tunnel

2 *Read the sentences. Write the sentence from the box that explains the underlined word.*

> I'm going to be late.
>
> ~~I work with a group of people.~~
>
> Our committee is going talk together today.
>
> There are a lot of cars on the road, and they are moving very slowly.
>
> We want to fix our traffic problems.
>
> Taking my car is not the easiest way for me to get to work.

1. I'm on a <u>committee</u>. There are 5 people on it.

   <u>I work with a group of people.</u>

2. The committee wants to find <u>solutions</u> to the city's traffic problems.

   _____

3. We have an important <u>meeting</u> this morning.

   _____

4. Unfortunately, the traffic is very <u>heavy</u> this morning.

   _____

5. Driving to work isn't always <u>convenient</u> for me.

   _____

6. I called my office to say that I am not going to be <u>on time</u> for the meeting.

   _____

3 READING ONE: Looking for Traffic Solutions

A. INTRODUCING THE TOPIC

You are going to read a memo about traffic. Before you read it, think about traffic. Check (✓) the words you think you will see in the memo. Share your answers with the class. Then read the memo.

_____ avoid   _____ increase   _____ pilot

_____ expert   _____ the Internet   _____ problem

TO: Traffic Solutions Committee, Austin, TX

FR: Rafael Torres, Staff Researcher

RE: Our next meeting

This committee is trying to find a solution to the traffic problem in Austin. Last month, I studied solutions from cities around the world. Please read this information before our next meeting.

Traffic Solutions in the United States

- Seattle, Washington, has bicycle lanes on many streets. Employees don't worry about traffic, and they feel healthy because they ride their bicycles.
- Atlanta, Georgia, is testing an Internet traffic map. It tells commuters where the traffic is heavy. Drivers can check the traffic on their computers at home.
- Connecticut has a "Deduct-a-Ride" program. If commuters and employers use buses or other public transportation instead of their cars, they pay lower taxes. Everyone is happy about saving money.
- Washington, D.C., has "high occupancy vehicle" (HOV) lanes. Cars with three or more people can use this special lane. Traffic moves much faster in HOV lanes.

Traffic Solutions Internationally

- In São Paolo, Brazil, some people use helicopters to get around the city. But most people can't take helicopters because helicopters are so expensive.
- Manila, Philippines, has a commuter train along the center of a major highway. Instead of driving, people ride the train. This seems like a good plan.
- Bangkok, Thailand, has a skytrain. It is 16 miles long. It is clean, fast, and on time. Traffic in Bangkok is better now. It isn't convenient for everyone because some people have to take a taxi to the skytrain.
- Cairo, Egypt, is building a tunnel under the city. The tunnel is for a new commuter train. The tunnel will take up less space in the city.

Can Austin use any of these solutions? Please think about this information carefully. We will discuss it at our next meeting on Monday at 10:00 A.M.

B. READING FOR MAIN IDEAS

Read the sentences. Check (✓) the main idea of Mr. Torres's memo.

Mr. Torres wants the committee to

_____ **1.** visit the cities in his report.

_____ **2.** think about the solutions from these cities.

_____ **3.** take public transportation more often.

C. READING FOR DETAILS

Match the place on the left with the traffic solution on the right.

Places	**Solutions**
_b_ **1.** Seattle, WA	**a.** helicopters
_____ **2.** Atlanta, GA	**b.** bicycle lanes
_____ **3.** Connecticut	**c.** Deduct-a-Ride
_____ **4.** Washington, DC	**d.** an Internet traffic map
_____ **5.** São Paolo, Brazil	**e.** commuter train along the highway
_____ **6.** Manila, Philippines	**f.** skytrain
_____ **7.** Bangkok, Thailand	**g.** HOV lanes
_____ **8.** Cairo, Egypt	**h.** tunnel for a commuter train

D. READING BETWEEN THE LINES

1 *Read Mr. Torres's memo again. Check (✓) the solutions Mr. Torres probably likes for Austin, Texas.*

_____ **1.** bicycle lanes

_____ **2.** helicopters

_____ **3.** Deduct-a-Ride program

_____ **4.** HOV lane

_____ **5.** skytrain

_____ **6.** commuter train along the highway

2 *Discuss your answers to Exercise 1 with the class. Complete these sentences.*

Mr. Torres likes this solution because _____.

Mr. Torres doesn't like this solution because _____.

READING TWO: | **Transportation Changes How We Do Business**

A. EXPANDING THE TOPIC

Read this newspaper article about the traffic problem in Austin, Texas. Then answer the question below.

Transportation Changes How We Do Business

Austin, TX—

Dell Computer Corporation, the biggest employer in Austin, is moving part of its company to the state of Tennessee.

Dell is moving for several reasons. One reason is the heavy traffic in Austin. Many employees have trouble getting to work because of the traffic.

Products also have to be on time. If products are late because of traffic, then customers will buy their computers from another company.

City leaders are looking for solutions to Austin's traffic problems. They want Dell and other large companies to stay in Austin.

Circle the best answer.

Why is Dell moving part of the company to Tennessee?

1. Dell's computers have problems.

2. People in Tennessee buy more computers than people in Texas.

3. There is less traffic in Tennessee than in Austin, TX.

B. LINKING READINGS ONE AND TWO

Look at Readings One and Two again. You are a member of Austin's Traffic Solutions Committee. Write a memo to the other members. Give your opinion of the best traffic solution for Austin. Give reasons for your opinion.

TO: Traffic Solutions Committee, Austin, TX

FR: _____, Committee Member
                     (your name)

RE: Possible Solutions to Austin Traffic

I read the report on traffic solutions. Here are my ideas.

I think _____ is the best solution to Austin's
traffic problems. I have two reasons.

First, _____

_____

_____

Second, _____

_____

_____

Companies like Dell Computer Corporation are very important for our city. We want _____

_____.

Please think about my suggestion. We can discuss my ideas at our meeting next week.

5 REVIEWING LANGUAGE

A. EXPLORING LANGUAGE

*Work with a partner. Look at these words from Readings One and Two. Write the words in the correct column. Some words can go in **both** columns.*

~~bicycle lanes~~	planes
buses	skytrains
cars	subways
commuter trains	taxis
helicopters	Internet traffic maps
HOV lanes	trucks
more highways	tunnels (for commuter trains)

FORMS OF TRANSPORTATION	TRAFFIC SOLUTIONS
	bicycle lanes

B. WORKING WITH WORDS

Read this information about Bangkok, Thailand. Then complete the paragraphs with the words from the list. Use each word only once.

cars	on time
commute	skytrain
commuters	solutions
heavy	~~traffic jams~~

Bangkok

Most people in Bangkok stay relaxed in <u>traffic jams</u>. "We
                                          1.

don't get upset," said one woman. "Getting upset will not change

anything. _____ traffic is a part of life here."
              2.

People in Bangkok plan on slow-moving traffic. Families often

_____ together. They leave home at 5:30 A.M. to get to
3.

school and to work _____. Some _____
4. 5.

work in their _____ while they sit in traffic. No one likes
6.

traffic, but people make the best of it.

The _____ helps a little, but the city of Bangkok is
7.

looking for more _____ to its traffic problem.
8.

6 SKILLS FOR EXPRESSION

A. GRAMMAR: Comparative Adjectives

1 *Work with a partner. Say these words to each other. Count the number of syllables in each word. For example, the word* easy *has two syllables (ea · sy). The word* small *has only one syllable. Write the number on the line.*

_1_ a. big

____ b. busy

____ c. expensive

____ d. noisy

____ e. old

2 *With your partner, read this information about the New York City subway and London's underground. Then write the answers in complete sentences. Follow the example.*

	New York City Subway	UNDERGROUND
Stations	468	248
Riders	3.5 million	2.7 million
Employees	26,000	16,000
Cost (fares)	U.S. $1.50	U.S. $1.90–$5.15
Hours open each day	24	20
Year opened	1904	1863

1. Which is bigger, the New York City subway or the London underground?

   The New York City subway is **bigger than** the London underground.

2. Which is busier?

   _____

3. Which is more expensive to ride?

   _____

4. Which is probably noisier?

   _____

5. Which is older?

   _____

3 *Look at the adjectives in the sentences on page 116. Then look at Exercise 1 on page 115. Answer these questions with your partner.*

1. Which adjective uses *more*? How many syllables does this adjective have?

2. Which adjectives add *-ier*? How many syllables did these adjectives have (before *-ier* was added)?

3. Which adjectives add *-er*? How many syllables did these adjectives have (before *-er* was added)?

Comparative Adjectives

FOCUS ON GRAMMAR

See comparative adjectives in *Focus on Grammar,* Introductory.

1. Use comparative adjectives to compare two people, places, or things.	
2. For adjectives with one syllable, add *-er*.	The subway is **bigger.** The subway is **cheaper.** An exception: fun → **more fun**
3. For adjectives with two or more syllables, use *more +* adjective.	The underground is **more expensive.** Some exceptions: quiet → **quieter** simple → **simpler**
4. For adjectives with two syllables that end in *y*, change *y* to *i* and add *-er*.	The subway is **busier.**
5. Use *than* when you are comparing two things in one sentence.	The underground is more expensive **than** the subway. The subway is busier **than** the underground.

4 *Work with a partner. Take turns asking questions about driving a car and walking to school. Write your partner's answers. Use the comparative form of the adjectives listed below. Then write a short paragraph about your partner's opinion.*

Your question

Which is faster, driving a car or walking?

Your partner's answer

1. Driving is faster than walking. _____ (fast)
2. _____ (cheap)
3. _____ (convenient)
4. _____ (fun)
5. _____ (dangerous)
6. _____ (quiet)
7. _____ (healthy)
8. _____ (relaxing)

Your partner's opinion

In general, _____ thinks _____
                    (your partner's name)   (driving a car/walking)

is better than _____ because _____
                    (driving a car/walking)

_____.

B. STYLE: Writing about Similarities

1 *Read these sentences about Main Street and State Street. Then answer the questions.*

Main Street is busy, and so is State Street.
Main Street is busy, and State Street is too.

Main Street has a lot of traffic, and so does State Street.
Main Street has a lot of traffic, and State Street does too.

1. When the verb in the first part of the sentence is a form of *be*, what is the verb in the second part?

2. When the verb in the first part of the sentence is a form of *have*, what is the verb in the second part?

Writing about Similarities

To show how things are the same, follow these patterns:	
Affirmative sentences with *be*:	Venice **is** beautiful, **and so is** Rome. Venice **is** beautiful, **and** Rome **is too**.
Affirmative sentences with other verbs:	Rio de Janeiro **has** a lot of tourists, **and so does** Beijing. John **takes** the bus to work, and Sofia **does too**.

2 *Read each pair of sentences about Taipei, Taiwan, and Los Angeles, California. Then combine each pair into one sentence. Write each answer in two different ways. Follow the example.*

1. The streets in Taipei are busy.
   The streets in Los Angeles are busy.

   a. The streets in Taipei are busy, and the streets in Los Angeles are too.

   b. The streets in Taipei are busy, and so are the streets in Los Angeles.

2. The traffic in Taipei is sometimes heavy.
   The traffic in Los Angeles is sometimes heavy.

   a. _____

   b. _____

3. Drivers in Taipei spend a lot of time in their cars.
   Drivers in Los Angeles spend a lot of time in their cars.

   a. _____

   b. _____

4. Traffic in Taipei often moves slowly.
   Traffic in Los Angeles often moves slowly.

   a. _____

   b. _____

5. Taipei is an exciting city.
   Los Angeles is an exciting city.

   a. _____

   b. _____

7 ON YOUR OWN

A. WRITING TOPICS

Choose one of the following writing topics. Use some of the vocabulary, grammar, and style from this unit.

1. Write a letter to a local government official. Tell the official about a specific traffic problem in your town or city. Suggest a solution.

2. Which do you prefer: taking a car or taking public transportation? Write a paragraph about your choice. Compare taking a car and taking public transportation. Give a reason for your answer.

3. Does traffic change your daily life in any way? In good ways? In bad ways? Write a paragraph about how traffic changes your life.

B. FIELDWORK

Most cities have traffic problems. How does your city or town control traffic?

1. What is the solution? To find information, look on the Internet, talk to a police officer, or call the traffic department in your city. Ask the following questions. Write the answers.
   a. What is the traffic problem?
   b. What is the solution?
   c. How does the solution help the city?

2. Write a paragraph about the problem and the solution. Begin your paragraph like this:

   _____ tries to control its traffic problems. For example, . . .
   (name of your city)

3. Share your writing with a partner. Read your partner's paragraph. Then do the following activities.
   a. Underline one sentence you do not understand. Ask your partner to explain this idea to you.
   b. Underline one sentence you think is very interesting. Tell your partner why you think it is interesting.

FULL HOUSE

1 APPROACHING THE TOPIC

A. PREDICTING

Look at the picture. Discuss these questions with the class.

1. How many children are there in this family?
2. How old are the children?
3. Do the children look alike?

B. SHARING INFORMATION

Look at the picture on page 121 again. The woman in the picture is Ellen Sullivan. Read Ellen's answers to the questions.

1. How many people are there in your family? What are their names?

   <u>There are five people in my family. There's me and my husband, Bob.</u>
   <u>We have three daughters: Kathryn, Kelly, and Heather.</u>

2. Are there any multiple births in your family? <u>Yes, there are. Kelly and</u>
   <u>Heather are twins. They were born on the same day.</u>

3. Where does your family live? <u>We live in Salem, Massachusetts.</u>

Now write your own answers to the questions above. Then ask a partner. Write your partner's answers.

Your answers

1. _____
2. _____
3. _____

Your partner's answers

1. _____
2. _____
3. _____

PREPARING
TO READ

A. BACKGROUND

Read the questions below and the chart on page 123. Fill in the missing numbers in the chart and answer question 5. Then share your answers with a partner.

1. How many total births were there in 1994?
2. How many multiple births were there in 1995?
3. How many quadruplets were born 1997?
4. How many twins were born in 1998?
5. Is the number of multiple births in the United States going up or down?

CHILDREN BORN IN THE UNITED STATES 1994–1998

Children	1994	1995	1996	1997	1998
Single births	3,841,109	3,797,880	3,784,805	3,770,020	3,823,258
Twins	97,064	96,736	100,750	104,137	_____
Triplets	4,233	4,551	5,298	6,148	6,919
Quadruplets	315	365	560	_____	627
Quintuplets and Sextuplets	46	57	81	79	79
Total multiple births	101,658	_____	106,689	110,874	118,295
Total births	_____	3,899,589	3,891,494	3,880,894	3,941,553

B. VOCABULARY FOR COMPREHENSION

Read the sentences. Then circle the definition of the underlined word.

1. We <u>donate</u> money and old clothes to the Red Cross, which gives it to people who need help.

    a. receive something because you need help
    b. give something to someone who needs help

2. My son sometimes feels angry or <u>jealous</u> when I spend a lot of time with my daughter.

    a. unhappy because someone is getting something you want
    b. thankful because you are getting something you want

3. When I go to my grandmother's house, she always gives me a big <u>hug</u> because she is happy to see me.

    a. putting your arms around someone to show love or friendship
    b. putting your hands together to show you like something

4. I passed my science test without studying! It's a <u>miracle</u>!

    a. something you want to do in the future; a goal
    b. something good that you think is not possible

5. My daughter is not really a bad child. She is just very <u>mischievous</u> sometimes.

    a. getting into trouble in small ways
    b. very intelligent; well educated

6. Mr. and Mrs. Garbo don't want to <u>raise</u> their children in the city. They think there are too many problems for kids in urban areas.

    a. send their children to school
    b. take care of children until they finish school

7. Terry and Pat have five children. They bought a <u>van</u> for their family because a regular car is too small.

    a. a large house with many rooms, like a hotel
    b. a large car with many seats, like a small bus

3

READING ONE: Seven Tiny Miracles

A. INTRODUCING THE TOPIC

1 *Read these headlines from newspapers and magazines. They are about one story. What do you think happened? Discuss these headlines with the class.*

Miracle in Iowa
—*Time* Magazine, 12/1/97

It's a Boy, Girl, Girl, Girl, Boy, Boy, Boy!
—*New York Post*, 11/20/97

IT'S A MIRACLE!
—*Time* Magazine, 12/1/97

2 *Read these sentences. Check (✓) your answers.*

	I think so.	I don't think so.	I'm not sure.
1. This story is about a baseball team.	____	____	____
2. This story is good news.	____	____	____
3. This story is about a big family.	____	____	____
4. This story is about a miracle.	____	____	____
5. This story happened in New York City.	____	____	____

Now read "Seven Tiny Miracles." Were your ideas correct?

Seven Tiny Miracles

1 *Des Moines, Iowa—(CCN)* On November 19, 1997, the number of people in Carlisle, Iowa, increased from about 3,400 to 3,407. It was a very historic day. Seven babies were born that day.

2 Kenny and Bobbi McCaughey (pronounced makóy) had a one-year-old daughter, and they wanted one or two more children. Unfortunately, Bobbi was having trouble becoming pregnant. Bobbi's doctor asked, "Do you want to try fertility drugs?"[1]

3 The doctor explained the risks of fertility drugs: The baby might not be healthy, or Bobbi might have a multiple birth. Kenny and Bobbi talked and prayed together. Then they decided to take the risk.

4 One month later, they went to see the doctor again. The doctor said, "You are going to have seven babies!" Everyone was surprised but also nervous. The doctor explained, "This is very dangerous. What do you want to do?" Kenny and Bobbi talked and prayed again. Then they said, "They are our children. We want them."

5 On November 19th Bobbi had the babies, two months early. Forty doctors and nurses helped Bobbi. In six minutes, she had four boys and three girls. They were the first living septuplets ever. Many people think they are a miracle.

6 It is not easy to raise eight children. Today the McCaugheys receive a lot of support from their family and people at their church. Every day six volunteers come for four hours between 8:00 A.M. and 5:00 P.M. They help cook, clean, and take care of the kids.

7 Many companies and other generous people also helped the McCaugheys. For example:
- Chevrolet, a car company, donated a new van for 12 people.
- The Gerber company donated baby food.
- Procter & Gamble, a diaper[2] company, donated Pampers.
- People from the community donated a new house with seven bedrooms.

8 Their life is not going to be easy, but the McCaugheys love all eight of their children. Each child is different.
- Mikayla is the oldest. Sometimes she feels jealous, but not usually.
- Alexis has the best smile.
- Brandon is mischievous.
- Joel loves hugs and kisses.
- Kelsey is very friendly.
- Kenny Jr. is energetic.
- Natalie is shy.
- Nathan has the best laugh.

9 Two of the septuplets have health problems, but Kenny and Bobbi are strong and want their family to be happy. Kenny and Bobbi are going to do their best.

---

[1] *fertility drugs:* medicine to help a woman become pregnant

[2] *diaper:*

B. READING FOR MAIN IDEAS

*Read each sentence. Write **T** (true) or **F** (false). Then write the number of the paragraph where you found your answer.*

Paragraph number

_____ 1. Sometimes it is dangerous to take fertility drugs. _____

_____ 2. Nobody was surprised about the septuplets. _____

_____ 3. The McCaugheys had the first living septuplets. _____

_____ 4. No one helps the McCaugheys. _____

C. READING FOR DETAILS

Read "Seven Tiny Miracles" again. Then complete the sentences with the correct numbers. Compare your numbers with your classmates' answers.

1. Before November 19th, the McCaugheys had ___one___ child.

2. Today, about _____ people live in Carlisle, Iowa.

3. Before they had the septuplets, the McCaugheys wanted to have _____ or _____ more children.

4. She gave birth to the septuplets _____ months early.

5. _____ doctors and nurses helped Bobbi.

6. Kenny and Bobbi have _____ sons and _____ daughters.

7. Mikayla has _____ brothers and _____ sisters.

8. Bobbi gave birth to the septuplets in only _____ minutes.

9. About _____ people can sit in the McCaugheys' new van.

10. Their new house has _____ bedrooms.

D. READING BETWEEN THE LINES

Look back at the reading. Then answer this question in complete sentences. Give your reasons.

Do Kenny and Bobbi McCaughey have a strong marriage?

4 READING TWO: The Dionne Quintuplets

A. EXPANDING THE TOPIC

The Dionne quintuplets

In 1934, the Dionne quintuplets were born. Multiple births were not common then. In 1997, three of the Dionne sisters wrote a letter to Kenny and Bobbi McCaughey.

Read the letter on page 129. It is similar to the letter that the Dionnes wrote to the McCaugheys.

November 1997

Dear Mr. and Mrs. McCaughey,

Congratulations on the birth of your beautiful children. We have a very special family, too. We want to tell you our story.

We were born on May 28, 1934, in a small town in Canada. Our family was poor. Our father thought, "Five daughters! If my daughters become famous, I can make a lot of money."

The government took us away from our family to protect[1] us from our father. Unfortunately, the government did not protect us. We lived in a special house called "Quintland." Every day, tourists came to look at us. We became very famous. The government made a lot of money, but we received very little money or love. We had a very unhappy life.

We hope your children will have happy lives. Please love and protect them always.

Sincerely,

Annette, Cécile, & Yvonne Dionne

---

[1] *protect*: to take care of; to keep someone away from danger

*Read each sentence. Write **T** (true), **F** (false) or **?** (if the information is not in the reading).*

_____ 1. The Dionne sisters became very rich.

_____ 2. The Dionne sisters became very famous.

_____ 3. The Dionnes think it is a good idea to take fertility drugs.

_____ 4. The Dionnes want the McCaugheys to protect their children.

B. LINKING READINGS ONE AND TWO

Congratulations! You are going to have sextuplets. Think about your family's future. Make two lists: "Do" and "Don't Do." Use the ideas below. Think about the McCaugheys and the Dionnes. What did you learn from their stories? Add some ideas of your own. Then discuss your lists with a partner.

ask people for help
buy a bigger house
~~buy a lot of diapers~~
call your friends
call the media
do TV interviews
dress the children in the same clothes
give the children names that sound similar
pray
protect the children from the media
quit your job
see a doctor
use the children to make money
write a book about the children

DO	DON'T DO
buy a lot of diapers	

5 REVIEWING LANGUAGE

A. EXPLORING LANGUAGE

Look at the box. It shows some important word forms. It does not give all the possible word forms. Then read each sentence and circle the correct word form.

Noun	Adjective	Verb
danger	dangerous	*
decision	*	decide
donation	*	donate
health	healthy	*
pregnancy	pregnant	*
risk	risky	risk
support	supportive	support

1. It can be _____ for a woman to have septuplets.

   a. danger
   b. (dangerous)

2. Parents need to make important _____ together.

   a. decisions
   b. decide

3. The Red Cross receives many _____ from generous people every day.

   a. donations
   b. donated

4. I was sick last week, but now I am _____.

   a. health
   b. healthy

5. When my mother was _____ with me, she gained 50 pounds.

    a. pregnancy

    b. pregnant

6. People must learn about the _____ before they take fertility drugs.

    a. risks

    b. risky

7. When I have problems, my family is always very _____.

    a. support

    b. supportive

B. WORKING WITH WORDS

Work with a partner. Write six sentences about the McCaughey family. Use some of the words below or use forms of these words from Section 5A. Put your sentences in time order. Then try to make a paragraph with your sentences.

Example

Many volunteers helped the McCaugheys with the babies.

advice
danger
decide
different
donate
fertility drugs
healthy
miracle
pregnant
risks
support
volunteer

6 SKILLS FOR EXPRESSION

A. GRAMMAR: Making Predictions with *be going to*

1 *Lisa and Harry are going to have a baby. They go to a fortune teller, Madame Lulu, to find out more about the baby. Read their conversation. Then answer the questions.*

LISA: Madame Lulu, <u>am</u> I <u>going to</u> have a baby boy or a baby girl? <u>Is</u> my baby <u>going to</u> be a doctor? A president?

LULU: Slow down! One question at a time. You <u>are going to</u> have a boy. No, wait . . . and a girl. No, wait . . .

LISA: Twins? <u>Am</u> I <u>going to</u> have twins?

LULU: No, you aren't. I see a boy, a girl, and another girl . . .

HARRY: What? <u>Are</u> we <u>going to</u> have triplets?

LULU: No, you <u>aren't going to</u> have triplets. I see . . .

HARRY: Wait! How many children <u>are</u> we <u>going to</u> have?

LULU: I see five. You <u>are going to</u> have five babies.

LISA: Quintuplets? That's wonderful! Isn't it?

HARRY: Oh my! What <u>are</u> we <u>going to</u> do?

LULU: That's $100, please.

1. Do the underlined words show _____?
   a. the past   **b.** the present   **c.** the future

2. What form of the verb comes after *be going to*?
   a. the present form   **b.** the base form   **c.** the past form

FOCUS ON GRAMMAR

See the future with *be going to* in *Focus on Grammar,* Introductory.

Making Predictions with *be going to*

Use *be going to* to make predictions about the future.

1. To make a prediction, use: *be* + *going to* + the base form of the verb	She **is going to have** a baby. We **are going to be** good parents.
2. To make negative predictions, use: *be* + *not* + *going to* + the base form of the verb	I **am not going to have** any children. You **are not (aren't) going to have** triplets.
3. To ask *yes/no* questions, use: *Be* + subject + *going to* + the base form of the verb	**Am I going to have** a boy? Yes, you are. No, you aren't. **Is my baby going to be** a doctor? Yes, she is. No, she isn't.
4. To ask *wh-* questions, use: *Wh-* word + *be* + subject + *going to* + the base form of the verb Note: If you do not know the subject of the question, use *is*.	**What are we going to do?** **Who are they going to see?** **What is going to happen?** **Who is going to help?**

2 *Write questions about the McCaugheys. Write three* yes/no *questions and three* wh- *questions. Use* **be going to.** *Then share your questions with the class and answer them together.*

Example

Are Kenny and Bobbi going to sleep a lot?

1. _____

2. _____

3. _____

Example

Where are they going to live?

4. _____

5. _____

6. _____

3 *Complete each sentence with the affirmative or negative form of* **be going to.**

In the future . . .

1. Bobbi and Kenny McCaughey __aren't going to__ sleep a lot.

2. They _____ pray a lot.

3. They _____ have a quiet house.

4. Bobbi and Kenny _____ have more kids.

5. They _____ change many diapers.

6. The McCaugheys _____ protect their children.

7. The McCaughey family _____ receive help from their friends.

8. Mikayla _____ receive a lot of attention.

9. She _____ play with her brothers and sisters.

10. The septuplets _____ go to college.

11. The seven kids _____ look alike when they are 50 years old.

B. STYLE: *Because*

1 *Match the first part of each sentence with the second part. Write the letter on the line.*

_____ 1. Bobbi McCaughey had seven babies . . .

_____ 2. Some women take fertility drugs . . .

_____ 3. People need to think about the risks . . .

_____ 4. Friends and family help Bobbi . . .

a. because they have trouble becoming pregnant.

b. because she took fertility drugs.

c. because it is difficult to take care of all the children at the same time.

d. because taking fertility drugs can be dangerous.

Because

Use *because* to give a reason. *Because* answers the question "Why?"

Why did Bobby McCaughey take fertility drugs?

Bobbi McCaughey took fertility drugs **because** she wanted to have another baby.

2 *Decide which sentence comes first. Then combine them into one sentence with* **because.** *Do not repeat the subject when you join the sentences. Use pronouns, if possible.*

1. The doctor was surprised.
   The doctor found seven babies, not just one.

   <u>The doctor was surprised because he found seven babies, not just</u>
   <u>one.</u>

2. The septuplets have very special parents.
   The septuplets are very lucky.

   _____

3. There are a lot of children in the McCaughey's house.
   The McCaugheys' house is usually noisy.

   _____

4. The Dionnes had a difficult life.
   People used the Dionnes to make money.

   _____

5. Many people help the McCaugheys.
   It isn't easy to raise eight children.

   _____

6. The Dionnes were worried about the septuplets' future.
   The Dionnes wrote the McCaugheys a letter.

   _____

3 *Do you want to be the parent of septuplets? Why or why not? Write your answer in one sentence with* **because.**

   _____

7 ON YOUR OWN

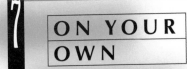

A. WRITING TOPICS

Choose one of the following writing topics. Use some of the vocabulary, grammar, and style from this unit.

1. What is Bobbi and Kenny McCaughey's future going to be like? Write a paragraph about their future. Use *be going to* in your sentences.

2. Are there any twins or triplets in your family or in a family you know? Write a paragraph about them. How are they alike? How are they different?

3. Write two paragraphs about someone in your family. In the first paragraph, describe this person today. What does he or she do? Use the simple present tense. In the second paragraph, predict what this person is going to be doing in 10 years. Use *be going to* in your second paragraph.

B. FIELDWORK

How much does it cost to have a child?

1. Imagine that you are the proud parent of a 10-year-old boy or girl. Look at the chart on page 138. Find out how much the items cost for one child for one year. Look on the Internet and visit stores. Add more items to the list. Then calculate the amount for the eight McCaughey children.

SUMMARY REPORT

Expenses for one year	For one child	For the eight McCaughey children
Haircut		
Visit to the doctor		
Lessons (piano, dance, karate, etc.)		
One pair of shoes		
Clothes (shirts, pants, dresses, underwear, pajamas, etc.)		
Computer game		
Toy or book		
Movie or video rental		
Other:_____		
_____		
_____		
Total		

2. Write a paragraph about how much it costs to raise children. Begin your paragraph like this: "Having children is expensive because . . ."

3. Share your summary report and writing with a partner. Read your partner's paragraph. Then answer these questions.

   a. Who has more items on the list, you or your partner?
   b. Who has higher prices, you or your partner? Are your partner's prices too high? Too low?
   c. Is there one sentence in your partner's paragraph that you do not understand? Underline it. Ask your partner to explain this idea to you.
   d. Is there one sentence in the paragraph that you think is very interesting? Underline it. Tell your partner why you think it is interesting.

IT'S YOUR LUCKY DAY

1 APPROACHING THE TOPIC

A. PREDICTING

Look at the pictures. Discuss these questions with the class.

1. What happened to this woman?
2. Was she lucky?
3. How does she feel?
4. Read the title of the unit. What does "It's Your Lucky Day" mean?

B. SHARING INFORMATION

1 *Congratulations! You just won $1,000,000. What will you do with the money? Look at the list below. Label each item.*

I = *important for you to do*
VI = *very important for you to do*
NI = *not important for you to do*

_____ **a.** Share the money with my family

_____ **b.** Get a new house or apartment

_____ **c.** Buy a new car

_____ **d.** Put the money in the bank

_____ **e.** Pay my telephone and credit card bills

_____ **f.** Pay for school

_____ **g.** Take a vacation

_____ **h.** Give the money to poor people

_____ **i.** Have a party

_____ **j.** Other ideas:_____

_____

Now compare your list with a partner's.

2 *Discuss your ideas with the class. What did most people say? What are the three most important things for people in your class?*

1. _____

2. _____

3. _____

Are any of the results surprising? Why or why not?

PREPARING TO READ

A. BACKGROUND

Read the information about the New Jersey State Lottery and study the graph. Then answer the questions on page 142. Share your answers with the class.

Where Does the Money Go?

Every day people in New Jersey benefit from the New Jersey Lottery. In 1999, New Jersey Lottery players received $888,000,000 in prizes. Stores that sold winning lottery tickets also received $90,000,000.

But everyone wins in the New Jersey Lottery. Every time you buy a lottery ticket, you help people in New Jersey. In 1999, 39 percent of money from tickets—that's $652,000,000—went to programs for education, at-risk teens, college scholarships, and support for the elderly and disabled.[1]

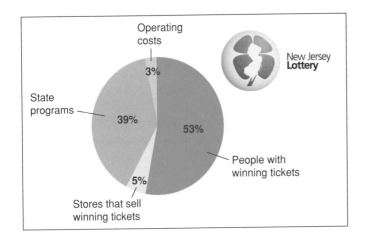

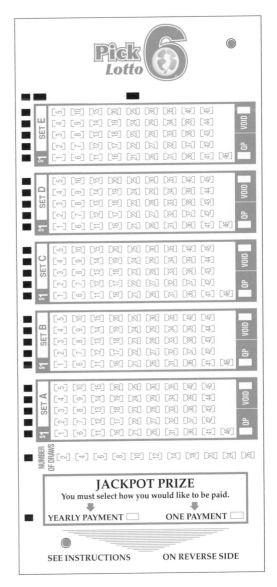

---

[1] *the elderly:* old people; *disabled:* people who cannot use part of their body properly

1. How does New Jersey use the money from lottery tickets? Check (✓) the correct answers.

New Jersey uses the money for

_____ education

_____ programs to help elderly and disabled people

_____ religious groups

_____ new highways

_____ operating costs

_____ vacations for politicians

_____ lottery prizes

_____ programs for at-risk teenagers

2. Give your opinion. Why do people buy lottery tickets? Write two reasons.

    a. _____

    b. _____

3. Discuss these questions with the class.
    a. Is there a lottery where you live?
    b. What do people in your community think about the lottery? Do they think the lottery is a good idea or a bad idea? Why?

B. VOCABULARY FOR COMPREHENSION

Read the sentences. Then circle the correct choice.

1. After Maria and Ted won $30,000, they <u>split</u> the money.
    a. Maria received all the money.
    b. Each person got some of the money.

2. There were seven children at the birthday party. Mrs. Harrington cut the birthday cake <u>evenly</u> into seven pieces.
    a. The pieces of cake were the same size.
    b. The pieces of cake were different sizes.

3. I called my brother last night, but he didn't answer. So, I <u>hung up</u> and tried again later.
    a. I waited a long time for my brother to answer the phone.
    b. I ended the first call and called at a different time.

4. Brenda told her sister a big secret. Then her sister told the secret to everyone at school. Brenda feels <u>betrayed</u> by her sister.

   a. Now Brenda can trust her sister.

   b. Now Brenda can't trust her sister

5. Frank gave his friend $100. His friend said, "I will give you the money back on Thursday." Frank said, "OK." But his friend <u>broke their agreement</u>.

   a. Frank got his money back on Thursday.

   b. Frank didn't get his money back on Thursday.

6. Gregory is very <u>greedy</u>. He always wants more of everything.

   a. Gregory tries to get money and other things for himself.

   b. Gregory tries to give money and other things to other people.

7. I played the lottery last week, and I <u>hit the jackpot</u>.

   a. I won $3,000,000.

   b. I won $3.

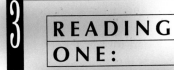

READING ONE: Sorry, Mom!

A. INTRODUCING THE TOPIC

There is an expression, "Money is the root[1] of all evil." What does it mean? Circle the correct answer.

a. Money is not important.

b. People with money are bad.

c. Money causes problems in life.

d. If you don't have money, you will have a difficult life.

---

[1] *root:*

Do you agree that "money is the root of all evil"? Circle the number that shows your opinion. Then discuss your ideas with the class.

Strongly agree   **Strongly disagree**

1   **2**   **3**   **4**   **5**   **6**

Now read this story about Jeffrey Johnson, a man who won the lottery. This is a true story. Think about how money changed Jeffrey's life.

Sorry, Mom!

1   Jeffrey Johnson, his wife, Bonnie, and their two sons live in Trenton, New Jersey. Jeffrey's parents, Joe and Barbara Johnson, also live in Trenton.

2   Jeffrey Johnson and his mother liked playing the lottery together. Every month they bought "Pick 6 Lotto" tickets in the New Jersey State Lottery. Every month for 10 years Jeffrey and his mother bought lottery tickets. They had an agreement: "If we have a winning ticket, we will split the jackpot evenly." They usually had losing tickets, but they enjoyed playing the lottery together.

3   Then, late at night on October 13th, Jeffrey called his mother on the telephone. He told her, "We won. We hit the jackpot! We have the winning ticket. The jackpot is $2,500,000!" Everyone in the Johnson family was very excited. Jeffrey said, "I'll call you tomorrow morning," and then he hung up the telephone.

4   The next day Jeffrey called his mother again. He said, "The winning ticket is not the ticket that you and I bought together. Bonnie and I bought the winning ticket together, so I am not going to split the money with you."

5   Now, Barbara is very upset. She feels betrayed by her son. She does not believe Jeffrey. She still loves her son, but she feels very hurt. She is going to sue[1] Jeffrey because she thinks he broke their agreement.

6   Jeffrey and Bonnie are very angry because Barbara wants half of the money. They feel betrayed because Barbara is going to sue Jeffrey. They think Barbara should accept the truth: She didn't win. They think Barbara is greedy. They do not want to speak to Barbara. In fact, on October 15th, Jeffrey and Bonnie changed their telephone number.

---

[1] *sue:* to take someone to a court of law because they hurt you in some way

B. READING FOR MAIN IDEAS

Imagine you are interviewing Jeffrey on October 15th. What does he say? First read each question. Then circle Jeffrey's answer.

Your questions   **Jeffrey's answers**

1. Did you buy any lottery tickets with your mother?   (Yes, I did.)   No, I didn't.

2. Did you buy any lottery tickets with your wife?   Yes, I did.   No, I didn't.

3. Did your mother hit the jackpot?   Yes, she did.   No, she didn't.

4. Are you going to split the jackpot with your mother?   Yes, I am.   No, I'm not.

5. Are you going to split the jackpot with your wife?   Yes, I am.   No, I'm not.

6. Does your mother believe your story about the winning ticket?   Yes, she does.   No, she doesn't.

C. READING FOR DETAILS

Answer each question in complete sentences.

1. For how long did Jeffrey and Barbara buy "Pick 6" tickets together?

   _____

2. How much money was the winning ticket worth?

   _____

3. What was the agreement between Jeffrey and Barbara?

   _____

4. What is Barbara going to do because of this situation?

   _____

5. How does Barbara feel about this situation?

   _____

6. How does Jeffrey feel about this situation?

   _____

D. READING BETWEEN THE LINES

What is your opinion about the situation between Barbara and Jeffrey? Read each sentence. Then check (✓) I agree or I disagree. Look back at the story to help you choose an answer. Discuss your answers with the class.

	I agree	I disagree
1. Jeffrey dreamed about becoming rich.	____	____
2. Money is very important to Barbara.	____	____
3. Barbara misunderstood when Jeffrey said, "We won!"	____	____
4. Jeffrey and his mother are going to buy lottery tickets together in the future.	____	____
5. Before Jeffrey won the lottery, the Johnsons were a happy family.	____	____

Discuss your opinion with the class. Do you believe Jeffrey? Do you believe Barbara?

4 READING TWO: Joe and Bonnie Put in Their Two Cents

A. EXPANDING THE TOPIC

The expression "to put in your two cents" means to give your opinion. Here Joe Johnson and Bonnie Johnson put in their "two cents." Read their opinions.

"You have to respect your mother! Your mother is more important than money. We don't want the money. We only care about our family. You told your mother, 'We won.' Then the next morning you called again and changed your story. We are upset because we don't understand what happened."

Joe Johnson, Jeffrey's father

**Bonnie Johnson,
Jeffrey's wife**

"It's not her money. She is not going to get any of it! We won the lottery honestly. Barbara misunderstood Jeffrey when he said, 'We won!' That's her problem, not ours. Now Barbara is suing her own son! It's unbelievable! Do you think we should be happy about that?"

*Read the sentences. Write **T** (true), **F** (false), or ? (if the information is not in the reading).*

_____ 1. Joe is upset with his son.

_____ 2. Joe wants Jeffrey to share the money with Barbara.

_____ 3. Joe thinks Jeffrey changed his story.

_____ 4. Bonnie wants to split the jackpot with her mother-in-law.

_____ 5. Bonnie is happy about this situation.

_____ 6. Bonnie plans to buy her mother-in-law an expensive gift.

B. LINKING READINGS ONE AND TWO

1 *Work with a partner. Read each sentence. Then decide who said it. Write **Jeffrey, Bonnie, Barbara,** or **Joe**. More than one answer is possible. Share your answers with the class.*

_____ 1. Family is more important than money.

_____ 2. I feel betrayed by my own mother!

_____ 3. Why did you change your phone number?

_____ 4. Why did you change your story?

_____ 5. When I said, "We won!" I meant Bonnie and me.

_____ 6. Your mother is very upset, and so am I.

_____ 7. Why do you want to sue me?

_____ 8. You can't have the money.

_____ 9. You told me, "We won!"

_____ 10. Your mother and I want to talk with you about this situation.

_____ 11. I'm sorry.

2 *After Jeffrey Johnson won the lottery, his parents invited Bonnie and him to a restaurant to talk about the situation. With your partner, write a conversation between these four people. Use some of the sentences from Exercise 1. Add your own sentences, too.*

Joe and Barbara are waiting in the restaurant. Then Jeffrey and Bonnie arrive.

JOE:	Hello, son.
BARBARA:	Hello, Jeff. Hello, Bonnie.
JEFFREY:	Hi. We're in a hurry. What do you want to say?

_____ : _____

_____ : _____

_____ : _____

_____ : _____

_____ : _____

_____ : _____

_____ : _____

5 REVIEWING LANGUAGE

A. EXPLORING LANGUAGE

1 *There are many expressions about money. Match the expression on the left with the meaning on the right.*

_e_ 1. Money is the root of all evil.

_____ 2. Money talks.

_____ 3. The best things in life are free.

_____ 4. Money doesn't grow on trees.

_____ 5. A penny saved is a penny earned.

a. Put money in the bank for the future, even a small amount of money.

b. People with a lot of money have power.

c. If you want to have money, you have to work hard.

d. Beautiful days and good friends do not cost any money.

e. Money causes problems in life.

2 *Steven and Adam are roommates. They are sitting in the kitchen, and they are talking about money. Read their conversations. Then fill in the correct expression about money from Exercise 1.*

1. STEVEN: Adam, I don't want to work. I think I'm going to quit my job and buy lottery tickets instead of working. What do you think of that?

ADAM: Steve, _____, you know. If you want money, you have to get a job and work. That's the only way!

2. ADAM: No vacation for us this year. We have to save money to pay for school.

STEVEN: That's OK, Adam. We can stay here this summer. Let's go to the beach and have picnics in the park. We don't have to spend a lot of money to have fun because

_____.

3. STEVEN: I saw a terrible story in the newspaper yesterday. A mother and her son were fighting over a winning lottery ticket.

ADAM: I saw that story, too. That *was* terrible! There are so many problems because of money. Do you think that

_____?

4. STEVEN: I can't believe people waste so much money on lottery tickets.

ADAM: I agree! Every week I put money in the bank. I always say, "_____!"

5. STEVEN: You know my friend Martina, right?

ADAM: Yeah. She won $1 million in the lottery last month. She's really lucky.

STEVEN: Right. Now, when she goes to a restaurant or to a store, they treat her like a queen! It's true:

_____!

B. WORKING WITH WORDS

Read the clues. Complete the crossword puzzle with words from the box.

agreement	jackpot	split
betrayed	respect	sue
excited	sorry	upset

Across

3. Now, everyone in the Johnson family feels very _____ about this situation.

5. Jeffrey Johnson hit the _____.

7. Barbara had an _____ with her son: "If we win, we will split the money evenly."

9. At first, Jeffrey felt very _____ about his winning ticket.

Down

1. Barbara said, "I can't believe it! I feel _____ by my son."

2. Jeffrey is not going to _____ the jackpot with Barbara.

4. When you apologize to someone, you say, "I'm _____."

6. Jeffrey's father believes that Jeffrey should _____ his mother.

8. Barbara plans to _____ her son because she thinks he broke their agreement.

6 SKILLS FOR EXPRESSION

A. GRAMMAR: *Should,* for Advice

1 *Steven won $500,000 in the lottery last week. He asks his roommate, Adam, for advice. Read their conversation. Then work with a partner and answer the questions.*

STEVEN: Adam, $500,000 is a lot of money! What should I do with it?

ADAM: Well, you should have some fun. You should spend some of it. You really should take a vacation in Europe or Mexico!

STEVEN: OK, but should I give my parents some money?

ADAM: Definitely. You should pay for school, too. But you shouldn't spend it all. Remember: "A penny saved is a penny earned." You should put some of your money in the bank. You will need it someday.

STEVEN: Yeah. You're right. So, when should we leave for Mexico?

1. What advice did Adam give to Steven? Make a list on a piece of paper. (*Hint:* Look for the word *should* or *shouldn't*.)

2. What form of the verb comes after *should*?

Should, for Advice

FOCUS ON GRAMMAR

See *should* for advice in *Focus on Grammar,* Introductory.

1. Use *should* to give someone advice. *Should* means "It's a good idea to . . ." Always use the base form of the verb after *should*.	You **should put** your money in the bank. **Base form** You really **should take** a vacation.
2. The negative of *should* is *should not*. Use *shouldn't* in speaking and informal writing. Always use the base form of the verb after *shouldn't*.	People **should not (shouldn't)** break an agreement. **Base form** You **shouldn't spend** all your money.
3. To ask *yes/no* questions, use: *Should* + subject + the base form of the verb	**Should we save** money to buy a new house? **Should Jeffrey apologize** to his mother?
4. To ask *wh-* questions, use: *Wh-* word + *should* + subject + the base form of the verb	**Why should I split** the money? **How much should Jeffrey give** to his mother?

2 *Complete the sentences with **should** or **shouldn't** and the base form of the verb. Follow the example. Compare your answers with a partner.*

1. Ben wants to buy a new house. He _____should play_____ the lottery.

                                 play

2. Bruce bought a lottery ticket yesterday. He _____ in the

                                                look

 newspaper to check the winning numbers.

3. Martina has a winning ticket. She and Linda always play the lottery

 together. They _____ the money evenly if they win.

                                split

4. Roger has another losing ticket. He isn't very lucky.

 _____ he _____ again?

                                             try

5. Sally wants to buy lottery tickets with her brother, Alan. She

 _____ it. It's too much trouble.

                  do

3 *Give advice. Read the problems and write sentences with **should** or **shouldn't**.*

1. My car isn't working. What should I do?

   _____

2. Laura just won $1,000 in the lottery. What should she do?

   _____

3. My brother wants to borrow $50. What should I do?

   _____

4. Bruce lives at home with his family for free. Bruce makes $500 a week at his job. How much should he put in the bank every month?

   _____

5. Martina wants a new motorcycle, but she only has enough money to buy an old one. What should she do?

   _____

6. Adam has $5,000. He wants to make a lot more money quickly. What should he do?

   _____

B. STYLE: Expressing an Opinion

1 *Read the question and opinions. Then answer the questions on page 154.*

Do you think people should play the lottery?

A: In my opinion, it is not OK to play the lottery. People who play the lottery are wasting their money.

B: I believe it is OK to play the lottery. Lotteries are good for the community.

C: I feel that people should not play the lottery. People should give their money to the elderly and disabled.

D: I think it is OK to play the lottery. People should do whatever they want with their money.

1. Which opinions say the lottery is good?

2. Which opinions say the lottery is bad?

3. What are four ways to express your opinion?

Expressing an Opinion

An opinion is your *belief* about something. When you write, you need to give your opinion in a clear way. You also need to support your opinion with clear, strong reasons because your reader might not have the same opinion as you.

Here are some ways to express an opinion:

In my opinion,
I believe (that)
I feel (that)   lotteries are good for the community.
I think (that)

To express a negative opinion use *do not (don't)* and the base form of the verb.

believe
I don't   feel   that money is the root of all evil.
think

2 *Read the questions and give your opinions. Write in complete sentences. Give reasons for your opinions. Use **because**, if possible.*

1. Are lotteries good or bad for a community?

   _____

   _____

2. Should Jeffrey Johnson split the money with his mother?

   _____

   _____

3. Should family members buy lottery tickets together?

   _____

   _____

ON YOUR OWN

A. WRITING TOPICS

Choose one of the following writing topics. Use some of the vocabulary, grammar, and style from this unit.

1. Do you think Jeffrey should split the jackpot with his mother?
   a. First, think of two or three good reasons on *both* sides of the argument. Write the reasons in the chart.

YES, HE SHOULD.	NO, HE SHOULDN'T.
1.	1.
2.	2.
3.	3.

   b. Next, choose *one* side. Answer the question above. Choose "Yes" or "No." Write your opinion in one paragraph.

2. What is going to happen next in the story of Jeffrey and his mother? Write the ending of the story in one paragraph. Use *be going to* when writing about the future.

3. Communities benefit from the lottery, but sometimes the lottery can cause trouble, too. Do you think it is a good idea to play the lottery? Write your opinion in one paragraph.

B. FIELDWORK

Think of a game.

1. Think of a game that you do not know how to play, for example, a card game, a board game, or a sport. Learn how to play it. Answer the questions. Write the rules of the game in order. Explain how a person wins this game and what kind of prize the winner receives.

   What is the name of the game?
   How do you play? What are the rules?
   How do you win?
   What does the winner get at the end?

2. Write a paragraph about this game. Use the answers to the questions above.

3. Share your writing with a partner. Read your partner's paragraph. Then explain your partner's game to the class. Ask your partner if you were correct.

ANSWER KEY

UNIT 1 ◆
THE FRIENDSHIP PAGE

1B. SHARING INFORMATION

1. the telephone
2. Answers will vary.

2A. BACKGROUND

① 1. The percentage of people in the United States who use the Internet
2. 15%
3. Answers will vary.

② 1. e-mailing (96%), reading the news (51%), and making travel plans (47%)
2. buying and selling stocks (6%), looking for a boyfriend or girlfriend (7%), and banking (20%)
3. Answers will vary.

2B. VOCABULARY FOR COMPREHENSION

1. b	6. b
2. a	7. a
3. a	8. a
4. b	9. b
5. a	

3A. INTRODUCING THE TOPIC

Answers will vary.

3B. READING FOR MAIN IDEAS

1. c
2. a

3C. READING FOR DETAILS

1. b	5. a
2. b	6. a
3. a	7. a
4. a	8. b

3D. READING BETWEEN THE LINES

Suggested answers:

1. T   They laughed at her idea.
2. F   She wants to make it friendlier.
3. T   Friends help her. She also meets people because of The Friendship Page.
4. T   People help her.
5. F   She probably thinks friendship is more important than money.

4A.   EXPANDING THE TOPIC

1. c
2. b
3. e
4. d
5. a

4B. LINKING READINGS ONE AND TWO

Suggested answers:

1. agree
2. agree
3. disagree
4. disagree
5. agree

5A. EXPLORING LANGUAGE

① **Nouns:**   advice, enemy, friend, friendship, goal, mirror, poetry, secret, volunteer, website
Adjectives: difficult, easy, fun, jealous, little, old, popular, young
Verbs: die, laugh, see, succeed, think, want, write
Note: *Fun* is also a noun (I like to have *fun*.).
Secret is also an adjective (I have a *secret* plan.)
Volunteer is also a verb (He *volunteers* at a school.)

② Answers will vary.

5B. WORKING WITH WORDS

1. goal	7. advice
2. friendship	8. poetry
3. laughed	9. popular
4. young	10. Volunteers
5. online	11. quotes
6. website	

6A. GRAMMAR

① 1. Q: <u>Is</u> the Friendship Page a website?
   A: Yes, it <u>is</u>. It <u>is</u> a website about friendship.
2. Q: Who <u>is</u> Bronwyn Polson?
   A: She <u>is</u> a young woman from Australia.
3. Q: <u>Am</u> I too young to help?
   A: No, you <u>aren't</u>.
4. Q: How old <u>is</u> The Friendship Page?
   A: It <u>is</u> three years old.

The verbs are *before* the subjects in questions.
The verbs are *after* the subjects in the answers.

2 1. Is The Friendship Page a website?
2. How old is The Friendship Page?
3. Who is Bronwyn Polson?
4. Is Bronwyn from England?
5. Where is Bronwyn from?
6. How old are you?
7. Where are you from?
8. Who are your best friends?

Your partner's answers (suggested)

1. Yes, it is (a website).
2. It is three years old.
3. She is a young woman from Australia.
4. No, she isn't. She is from Australia.
5. She is from Australia.
6. I am ___ years old. (or: "I'd rather not say.")
7. I am from ___ [place].
8. My best friends are ___ [names].

6B. STYLE

1 7

2 **What is Tintota?**

Tintota is another website about friendship. It's great! Friends chat together and help each other on this website. Warren and Sylvia Roff-Marsh started Tintota. Like Bronwyn Polson, they live in Australia. Friendship is important to them.

Do you want more information about Tintota? Visit Tintota's website at www.tintota.com.

3 Answers will vary.

UNIT 2 ◆ ART FOR EVERYONE

2A. BACKGROUND

1 1. F   3. T
2. F   4. T

2 Answers will vary.

2B. VOCABULARY FOR COMPREHENSION

1. Energetic   7. painting
2. famous   8. sculpture
3. gallery   9. upset
4. museum   10. graffiti
5. ad   11. drawing
6. public

3A. INTRODUCING THE TOPIC

Suggested answers: for 32 years (1958–1990), for 18 years (1978–1990), or for 12 (1982–1990)

3B. READING FOR MAIN IDEAS

1. a
2. c
3. a

3C. READING FOR DETAILS

1. energy
2. graffiti
3. public
4. ads
5. decide
6. Social issues
7. money

3D. READING BETWEEN THE LINES

Answers will vary.

4A. EXPANDING THE TOPIC

1. Answers will vary.
2. Suggested answer: They all have simple, dark lines.
3. Suggested answer: The pictures on page 20 are about life (more general). They do not have words in them. The pictures on page 26 are about social issues (more specific). They have words in them.

4B. LINKING READINGS ONE AND TWO

Suggested answers:

IDEAS IN HARING'S ART	Untitled, 1984	Radiant Baby	Pop Shop NYC Logo	Stop AIDS	Free South Africa
Politics				✓	✓
AIDS				✓	
Love	✓	✓			
Energy	✓	✓	✓	✓	✓
Freedom				✓	✓
Children		✓			
Fear	✓			✓	✓

5A. EXPLORING LANGUAGE

1 1. +   5. +
2. −   6. −
3. +   7. −
4. −

2 Answers will vary.

5B. WORKING WITH WORDS

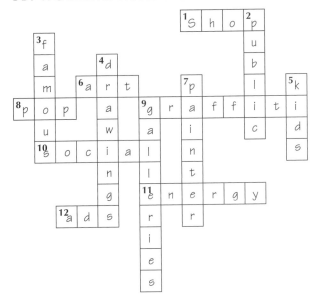

6A. GRAMMAR

1 AW: <u>Was</u> Haring different from other artists?
ER: Yes, he <u>was</u>.

AW: How <u>was</u> he different?
ER: Haring liked to make art in public places, like in the subway. He believed, "Art is for everyone." First, he <u>was</u> famous for his public art. Later, he became famous in galleries and museums.

He <u>was</u> also different because his paintings and drawings <u>were</u> in magazine ads. His art <u>was</u> on other things such as Swatch watches. He also sold his art in the Pop Shop. He used his art in unusual ways to communicate with the world.

- *was* 6; *were* 1
- We use *am, is,* and *are* to show present time. We use *was* and *were* to show past time.

2
1. were	6. were
2. were	7. was
3. weren't, was	8. was
4. was	9. was, wasn't
5. was	10. were

3
1. Who was Keith Haring?
2. Was Haring famous in the 1970s?
3. In what city was Haring born?
4. Was Haring only a painter?

5. Were his drawings controversial?
6. Where were the two Pop Shops?
7. How old was Keith Haring in 1990?

Your partner's answers (suggested)

1. Keith Haring was an artist in the 1980s.
2. No, he wasn't. He was famous in the 1980s.
3. He was born in Kutztown, PA.
4. No, he wasn't. He was also a sculptor and a graffiti artist.
5. His art was controversial because it was about social issues.
6. They were in New York City and Tokyo.
7. He was 32 (years old).

6B. STYLE

1
1. Keith Haring was born on May 4⌒1958.
2. Haring lived in Knokke⌒Belgium in 1987.
3. He liked to paint⌒draw⌒and sculpt.
4. Haring's art was funny⌒but it was also serious.
5. He also made commercial art. For example⌒ he made ads for magazines.

a. 5
b. 1
c. 4
d. 2
e. 3

2

The Haring Family

Keith Haring was born in Kutztown, PA. He lived with his mother, his father, and his three sisters. His sisters' names were Kay, Karen, and Kristen. Keith liked Kay and Karen, but Kristen was probably his favorite. Kristen was the baby in the family. She was 12 years younger than Keith. Keith and Kristen were always good friends.

Tokyo Pop Shop

Haring opened a Pop Shop in Tokyo on January 30, 1988. He wanted the Tokyo Pop Shop to be successful, but it had many problems. People did not buy Haring's art at the Tokyo Pop Shop because there were cheap copies everywhere. For example, you could buy T-shirts, pins, and posters with "fake" Haring art on them. Finally, the Pop Shop in Tokyo closed in 1989.

UNIT 3 ◆
WHAT'S IT WORTH TO YOU?

2A. BACKGROUND

1. No, it isn't. There are similar shows in other countries.
2. Answers will vary.

2B. VOCABULARY FOR COMPREHENSION

a. expert
b. secret
c. sentimental value
d. educational
e. rare
f. items
g. condition
h. is worth

3A. INTRODUCING THE TOPIC

Answers will vary.

3B. READING FOR MAIN IDEAS

1. false (2, 4)
2. true (3)
3. false (4)
4. false (5)

3C. READING FOR DETAILS

1. e (para 2)
2. c (para 3)
3. a (para 5)
4. d (para 5)
5. b (para 6)
6. f (para 7)

3D. READING BETWEEN THE LINES

Suggested answers: 1, 4, 5, 6

4A. EXPANDING THE TOPIC

a. 2
b. 4
c. 1
d. 3

4B. LINKING READINGS ONE AND TWO

1. expert, d
2. guest, i
3. expert, a
4. expert, f
5. guest, e
6. guest, b
7. expert, h
8. expert, c
9. expert, g

5A. EXPLORING LANGUAGE

Nouns: collection, collector, condition, education, excitement, expert, guest, history, item, secret, value
Adjectives: collectible, common, educational, exciting, favorite, historical, rare, sentimental, valuable
Note: *Secret* is also an adjective (I have a *secret* plan.). *Collectible* is also a noun (That gift shop sells *collectibles*.).

5B. WORKING WITH WORDS

1. valuable
2. condition
3. antique
4. worth
5. collect
6. collection
7. collector
8. rare
9. sentimental
10. value
11. history
12. favorite
13. expert

6A. GRAMMAR

1   I <u>am</u> a sports writer and I <u>love</u> my job because I <u>love</u> sports, especially football and baseball. But I <u>have</u> a secret.

Every Monday night I <u>watch</u> my favorite TV show. Sometimes the telephone <u>rings</u>, but I <u>don't</u> <u>answer</u> it. I <u>tell</u> my friends that I <u>watch</u> *Monday Night Football,* but that <u>isn't</u> true.

1. ten
2. don't answer, isn't
3. b

2
1. do . . . have
2. have
3. remember
4. wear
5. Do . . . wear
6. do
7. take
8. do . . . know
9. don't know
10. doesn't think
11. is
12. Does . . . look
13. is
14. is not (isn't)
15. is
16. love
17. plan
18. want
19. has

6B. STYLE

1
1. The first sentence.
2. The writer continues on the same line.
3. The writer stops at the right margin and moves to the next line.

Paragraph 1

In 1997, a man named Russ Pritchard was a guest on <u>Antiques Roadshow.</u> He had a large sword. When he was young, Pritchard found the sword in his new house. George Juno, an antiques expert, told Pritchard it was an American Civil War sword. Juno said the sword was very rare and worth $35,000. Pritchard was very surprised to hear this.

Paragraph 2

> On March 31, 2000, there was a story in the newspaper about Pritchard and Juno. WGBH, a Boston TV station, learned that Pritchard's story was not true. Pritchard and Juno had made up the story together. WGBH was very angry because it wants only true stories on <u>Antiques Roadshow</u>. As a result, Juno cannot be on <u>Antiques Roadshow</u> in the future.

UNIT 4 ◆
STRENGTH IN NUMBERS

2A. BACKGROUND

1. They are helpful.
2. Answers will vary.

2B. VOCABULARY FOR COMPREHENSION

a. 8
b. 6
c. 1
d. 2
e. 3
f. 9
g. 7
h. 4
i. 10
j. 11
k. 5

3A. INTRODUCING THE TOPIC

1. Hurt in car accidents involving alcohol
2. Have babies
3. Arrested for drugs
4. Arrested for violent crimes
5. Hurt by guns
6. Start smoking
7. Killed by guns

3B. READING FOR MAIN IDEAS

Sentences 2, 4, 5

3C. READING FOR DETAILS

1. c
2. d
3. f
4. h
5. b
6. g
7. a
8. e

3D. READING BETWEEN THE LINES

Suggested answers: 1, 2, 7, 9

4A. EXPANDING THE TOPIC

1. b
2. b
3. a

4B. LINKING READINGS ONE AND TWO

Answers will vary.

5A. EXPLORING LANGUAGE

1. support   *Start* and *begin* are synonyms and so are *help* and *support*.
2. dangerous   *Strength* is the noun form of the adjective *strong*, and *danger* is the noun form of the adjective *dangerous*.
3. positive   *Lazy* and *energetic* are opposites (antonyms), and so are *negative* and *positive*.
4. teenager   *Ad* is the short form of *advertisement*, and *teen* is the short form of *teenager*.
5. respect   *Dislike* and *like* are opposites, and so are *disrespect* and *respect*.
6. nickname   *Bob* is a nickname for *Robert*.
7. generous   Someone who always *takes* is *greedy*, and someone who always *gives* is *generous*.
8. crime   Baseball *teams* plays *baseball* together. *Gangs* are involved in *crime*. *Crime* is what the members do together.

5B. WORKING WITH WORDS

1. teenagers
2. at-risk
3. avoid
4. crime
5. role models
6. teach
7. members
8. positive
9. support

6A. GRAMMAR

1 1. they
2. them
3. their

2 1. he
2. He, his
3. he, he
4. him
5. he, he
6. him, his
7. he
8. He
9. him
10. He
11. he, his, him, his
12. He

(3)
1. She
2. her
3. her
4. She
5. She
6. her
7. her
8. They
9. her
10. he
11. he
12. her
13. Her
14. she
15. her
16. she
17. them

6B. STYLE

(1)

Greeting
Date
(Today's date)
Dear (Your friend's name)
Hi. How are you doing? I'm fine, but I miss you.
This year I joined the Urban Angels. I'm really excited about it.
After school and on weekends, Urban Angels _____
_____. For example, we _____
Message _____
_____.
I like being an Urban Angel because _____
_____. I am learning to _____
_____
If you move back to New York, I hope you will join Urban Angels, too.
I hope you are having fun in school this year. Write back soon.
Closing
Best regards,
Signature
Your name

(2) Answers will vary.

UNIT 5 ◆
GOING OUT OF BUSINESS

2A. BACKGROUND

Suggested answers:

1. Stamford has beautiful homes, friendly neighbors, parks and gardens, great public schools, public golf courses, family-owned businesses, the University of Connecticut, beaches, theaters, and restaurants.
2. Stamford has hotels, public golf courses, family-owned businesses, large corporations, theaters, and restaurants. It is also 50 minutes from New York City.
3. Answers will vary.

2B. VOCABULARY FOR COMPREHENSION

(1)
1. d
2. c
3. g
4. b
5. f
6. a
7. e

(2) Suggested answers:
1. I can buy books or magazines at a bookstore.
2. You can get a haircut at a barbershop.
3. She gets medicine at a drugstore.
4. I rent movies at the video store on Main Street.
5. I buy pens, pencils, and paper at an office supply store.
6. I want to buy a TV, CD player, or VCR at this electronics store.
7. You can get materials and tools to build a new house at the hardware store.

(3)
a. benefit
b. discount
c. owner
d. loyal
e. customers
f. increase
g. compete
h. employee
i. selection

3A. INTRODUCING THE TOPIC

Suggested answers: expert, goal, online, rare, service, support

3B. READING FOR MAIN IDEAS

1. b
2. a
3. b
4. a
5. b

3C. READING FOR DETAILS

1. a
2. a
3. c
4. c
5. d
6. a
7. b

3D. READING BETWEEN THE LINES

Suggested answers:
1. T
2. T
3. F
4. T
5. F
6. T

4A. EXPANDING THE TOPIC

1. 2 million
2. 78,000, 15,000
3. 26
4. 5,700, 2,000
5. two
6. 38 million
7. 10,000–14,000
8. 700
9. 1,500

4B. LINKING READINGS ONE AND TWO

Suggested answers:

1. CV
2. B
3. B
4. B
5. BB
6. CV
7. BB
8. BB
9. B

5A. EXPLORING LANGUAGE

1. competitors
2. compete
3. competition
4. employs
5. employees
6. loyal
7. loyalty
8. increase (verb)
9. increase (noun)
10. serves
11. service
12. owns
13. owner

5B. WORKING WITH WORDS

1. bookstore
2. owner
3. chain
4. competitors
5. loyal
6. selection
7. discounts
8. customers
9. service
10. business

6A. GRAMMAR

May 15th

1 Dear Sofia,

How are you? I miss you, and I miss school. But I am happy to be back in Seoul, too.

Seoul is different now. I am really upset about one change. Soon they are going to put a McDonald's restaurant on my beautiful street! There was a flower shop there before. I can't believe it!

My neighborhood is near Yonsei University in Seoul. It is very quiet here. There are a lot of students and professors in my neighborhood. There are also many family-owned businesses on the main street. There is a flower shop. Also, there are two video stores, a bakery, a vegetable shop, and a clothing store. But there aren't any large chain stores, and there isn't a McDonald's. Not yet! I don't want my neighborhood to change.

I hope you are OK. Can you visit Korea soon? We can go to McDonald's together. Just kidding.

Love,
Young-Hee

1. *there is* (1), *there isn't* (1), *there are* (3), *there aren't* (1)
2. video stores, McDonald's. Here *McDonald's* means "a McDonald's restaurant."
3. students, businesses, stores

2
1. are
2. are
3. are
4. wasn't
5. are
6. are
7. was
8. is
9. is
10. Is

3 Answers will vary.

6B. STYLE

2 Answers will vary.

UNIT 6 ◆ FLYING HIGH AND LOW

1B. SHARING INFORMATION

1
1. Richard Nixon
2. Marilyn Monroe
3. Nelson Mandela
4. Christopher Reeve
5. Vincent van Gogh
6. Pu Yi
7. Diana Spencer

2 Answers will vary.

2A. BACKGROUND

2
1. Raymond Orteig
2. $25,000
3. non-stop
4. Atlantic
5. New York (Paris)
6. Paris (New York)

2B. VOCABULARY FOR COMPREHENSION

1. handsome
2. pilot
3. took off
4. contest
5. landed
6. set a record
7. flight
8. hero
9. media

3A. INTRODUCING THE TOPIC

Suggested answers:

The weather was bad.

The plane was too small to cross the ocean.

The trip was too long.

3B. READING FOR MAIN IDEAS

1. b   2. b   3. a   4. c

3C. READING FOR DETAILS

Suggested answers:
1. Lindbergh was 25 years old when he flew across the Atlantic.

2. He took off from New York on the 20th of May.
3. He took off from New York at 7:52 A.M.
4. One person was on Lindbergh's plane when he flew across the Atlantic.
5. Lindbergh's flight was 3,610 miles (long).
6. He was in the air for 33½ hours.
7. He took five sandwiches on his trip.
8. He landed in Paris on the 21st of May.
9. About 150,000 people greeted him when he arrived in Paris.

3D. READING BETWEEN THE LINES
Answers will vary.

4A. EXPANDING THE TOPIC
1 Suggested answers: He was a pilot, husband, unofficial diplomat, airplane inspector, father, adventurer, inventor, writer/author, environmentalist, hero, enemy.

2 Answers will vary.

4B. LINKING READINGS ONE AND TWO
Suggested answers:

High Points

He set flying records.

He won Orteig's contest.

He met presidents, kings, and queens from around the world.

He was *Time* magazine's Man of the Year.

He married Anne Morrow, and they had several children.

He invented an "artificial heart."

He won the Pulitzer Prize.

Low Points

His first son was kidnapped.

He had to take his family to England to escape the media.

People called him "anti-American."

He had cancer.

5A. EXPLORING LANGUAGE
1. took off
2. landed
3. solo
4. handsome
5. contest
6. media
7. famous
8. flight
9. pilot

5B. WORKING WITH WORDS
1. pilot
2. flying
3. flight
4. famous
5. solo
6. took off
7. landed
8. plane

6A. GRAMMAR
1 1. kidnapped, asked, arrested, died
2. left, paid, found, was, said
3. Use *did* + *not* + the base form of the verb (didn't do, did not believe, did not kidnap).

2
1. started
2. wanted
3. wanted
4. tried
5. was
6. was
7. died
8. did
9. arrived
10. called
11. became
12. was
13. didn't change
14. had
15. wasn't
16. didn't want
17. thought
18. was
19. didn't agree
20. didn't think
21. was

3 Answers will vary.

6B. STYLE
1
a. 4
b. 6
c. 5
d. 2
e. 3
f. 1
g. 7

2 Suggested answers:
1. First,
2. Then,
3. Next,
4. Finally,

3 Answers will vary.

4 Answers will vary.

UNIT 7 ◆
ARE WE THERE YET?

2A. BACKGROUND
1. the increases in driving in the United States
2. the increase in the number of people who live farther away from their jobs
3. the increase in car trips
4. 17%

2B. VOCABULARY FOR COMPREHENSION
1
1. tunnel
2. train
3. helicopter
4. highway
5. commuter
6. lanes
7. subway

2 1. I work with a group of people.
2. We want to fix our traffic problems.
3. Our committee is going to talk together today.
4. There are a lot of cars on the road, and they are moving very slowly.
5. Taking my car is not the easiest way for me to get to work.
6. I'm going to be late.

3A. INTRODUCING THE TOPIC

Suggested answers: avoid, expert, increase, problem

3B. READING FOR MAIN IDEAS

2

3C. READING FOR DETAILS

1. b
2. d
3. c
4. g
5. a
6. e
7. f
8. h

3D. READING BETWEEN THE LINES

1 Suggested answers: 1, 3, 4, 6

2 Answers will vary.

4A. EXPANDING THE TOPIC

3

4B. LINKING READINGS ONE AND TWO

Answers will vary.

5A. EXPLORING LANGUAGE

Suggested answers:

Forms of Transportation: buses, cars, commuter trains, helicopters, planes, skytrains, subways, taxis, trucks

Traffic Solutions: bicycle lanes, commuter trains, HOV lanes, more highways, skytrains, Internet traffic maps, tunnels for commuter trains

5B. WORKING WITH WORDS

1. traffic jams
2. Heavy
3. commute
4. on time
5. commuters
6. car
7. skytrain
8. solutions

6A. GRAMMAR

1 a. 1
b. 2
c. 3
d. 2
e. 1

2 1. The New York City subway is bigger than the London underground.
2. The New York City subway is busier than the London underground.
3. The London underground is more expensive than the New York City subway.
4. The New York City subway is probably noisier than the London underground.
5. The London underground is older than the New York City subway.

1. expensive, 3
2. busy, noisy, 2
3. big, old, 1

4 Suggested answers:
1. Which is faster, driving a car or walking? Driving is faster than walking.
2. Which is cheaper, driving a car or walking? Walking is cheaper than driving.
3. Which is more convenient, driving a car or walking?
Driving is more convenient than walking.
4. Which is more fun, driving a car or walking? Driving is more fun than walking.
5. Which is more dangerous, driving a car or walking?
Driving is more dangerous than walking.
6. Which is quieter, driving a car or walking? Walking is quieter than driving.
7. Which is healthier, driving a car or walking? Walking is healthier than driving.
8. Which is more relaxing, driving a car or walking?
Walking is more relaxing than driving.

6B. STYLE

1 1. a form of *be*
2. a form of *do*

2 1. a. The streets in Taipei are busy, and the streets in Los Angeles are too.
b. The streets in Taipei are busy, and so are the streets in Los Angeles.
2. a. Traffic in Taipei is sometimes heavy, and traffic in Los Angeles is too.
b. Traffic in Taipei is sometimes heavy, and so is traffic in Los Angeles.

3. a. Drivers in Taipei spend a lot of time in their cars, and drivers in Los Angeles do too.
   b. Drivers in Taipei spend a lot of time in their cars, and so do drivers in Los Angeles.
4. a. Sometimes traffic in Taipei moves slowly, and traffic in Los Angeles does too.
   b. Sometimes traffic in Taipei moves slowly, and so does traffic in Los Angeles.
5. a. Taipei is an exciting city, and Los Angeles is too.
   b. Taipei is an exciting city, and so is Los Angeles.

UNIT 8 ◆
FULL HOUSE

2A. BACKGROUND
1. 3,942,767
2. 101,709
3. 510
4. 110,670
5. It is going up.

2B. VOCABULARY FOR COMPREHENSION
1. b
2. a
3. a
4. b
5. a
6. b
7. b

3A. INTRODUCING THE TOPIC
② Answers will vary.

3B. READING FOR MAIN IDEAS
1. T (3)
2. F (4)
3. T (5)
4. F (6, 7)

3C. READING FOR DETAILS
1. one
2. 3,400 (or 3,407)
3. one, two
4. two
5. Forty
6. four, four
7. four, three
8. six
9. 12
10. seven

3D. READING BETWEEN THE LINES
Suggested answers:
• Yes, they do. They are both happy with their big family. They accepted the responsibility for their big family together. They prayed together before making their difficult decisions.

• No, they don't. With so many children, they have no time to spend together alone. They are too busy to have a close relationship.

4A. EXPANDING THE TOPIC
② 1. F
   2. T
   3. ?
   4. T

4B. LINKING READINGS ONE AND TWO
Suggested answers:

Do: buy a lot of diapers, ask people for help, buy a bigger house, call your friends, pray, protect the children from the media, see a doctor, write a book about the children

Don't Do: call the media, do TV interviews, dress the children in the same clothes, give the children names that sound similar, quit your job, use the children to make money

5A. EXPLORING LANGUAGE
1. b
2. a
3. a
4. b
5. b
6. a
7. b

5B. WORKING WITH WORDS
Answers will vary.

6A. GRAMMAR
① 1. c
   2. b
② Answers will vary.
③ Suggested answers:
   1. are not going to
   2. are going to
   3. aren't going to
   4. aren't going to
   5. are going to
   6. are going to
   7. is going to
   8. is going to
   9. is going to
   10. are going to
   11. aren't going to

6B. STYLE
① 1. b
   2. a
   3. d
   4. c
② 1. The doctor was surprised because he found seven babies, not just one.
   2. The septuplets are very lucky because they have very special parents.
   3. The McCaughey's house is usually noisy because there are a lot of children in it.

4. The Dionnes had a difficult life because people used them to make money.
5. Many people help the McCaughey's because it isn't easy to raise eight children.
6. The Dionnes wrote the McCaugheys a letter because they were worried about the septuplets' future.

3 Answers will vary.

UNIT 9 ◆
IT'S YOUR LUCKY DAY

2A. BACKGROUND
1. education, programs to help elderly and disabled people, operating costs, lottery prizes, programs for at-risk teens
2. Answers will vary.
3. Answers will vary.

2B. VOCABULARY FOR COMPREHENSION
1. b   5. b
2. a   6. a
3. b   7. a
4. b

3A. INTRODUCING THE TOPIC
c

3B. READING FOR MAIN IDEAS
1. Yes, I did.   4. No, I'm not.
2. Yes, I did.   5. Yes, I am.
3. No, she didn't.   6. No, she doesn't.

3C. READING FOR DETAILS
Suggested answers:
1. They bought "Pick 6" lottery tickets together for ten years.
2. The winning ticket was worth $2,500,000.
3. The agreement was "if we have a winning ticket, we will split the jackpot evenly."
4. Barbara is going to sue Jeffrey.
5. She feels upset, betrayed, and hurt.
6. He feels angry and betrayed.

3D. READING BETWEEN THE LINES
Suggested answers:
1. I agree. (He played the lottery for many years.)
I disagree. (He wanted to do something fun with his mother.)

2. I agree. (She is fighting with her son over the jackpot.)
I disagree. (She doesn't care about the money, but she thinks Jeffrey is not telling the truth.)
3. I agree. (She thought "we" meant "Jeffrey and Barbara.")
I disagree. (She thought "we" meant "Jeffrey and Bonnie.")
4. I agree. (They are going to apologize and start playing the lottery together again.)
I disagree. (They are going to play separately. Also, perhaps Jeffrey doesn't need to play the lottery. He has a lot of money now.)
5. I agree. (They played the lottery together, and they seemed happy.)
I disagree. (If they had been happy before, they would not fight about money now.)

4A. EXPANDING THE TOPIC
1. T   4. F
2. ?   5. F
3. T   6. ?

4B. LINKING READINGS ONE AND TWO
1 Suggested answers:
1. Joe, Barbara   7. Jeffrey
2. Jeffrey   8. Bonnie, Jeffrey
3. Barbara, Joe   9. Barbara
4. Barbara, Joe   10. Joe
5. Jeffrey   11. everyone
6. Joe

2 Answers will vary.

5A. EXPLORING LANGUAGE
1 1. e   4. c
2. b   5. a
3. d

2 1. money doesn't grow on trees
2. the best things in life are free
3. money is the root of all evil
4. A penny saved is a penny earned
5. money talks

5B. WORKING WITH WORDS

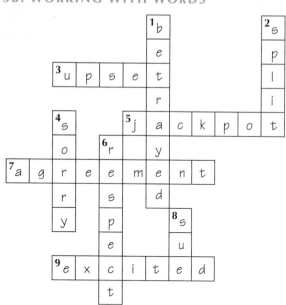

Crossword:

3 across: upset
5 across: jackpot
7 across: agreement
9 across: excited

Down clues (letters shown): b/e/t/r (1), s/p/l/i/t (2), s/o/r/r/y (4), j (5), r/e/s/p/e/c/t (6), s/u (8)

6A. GRAMMAR

1 1. Adam says:
Steven should spend some of it.
He should take a vacation.
He should have some fun.
He should give some of it to his parents.
He should pay for school.
He shouldn't spend all of it.
He should put some of it in the bank.
2. the base form

2 1. should play
2. should look
3. should split
4. Should . . . try
5. shouldn't do

3 Answers may vary.

6B. STYLE

1 1. B, D
2. A, C
3. In my opinion, I believe, I feel that, I think

2 Answers will vary.

Text Credits

Pages 2, 3, "How Americans Communicate" and "Percentage of People Online" bar graph data from *Time* Magazine, Aug. 9, 1999; **pp. 6, 7, 10**, Readings One and Two from The Friendship Page (www.friendship.com.au); **p. 40**, Reading Two, "Collecting Today for Tomorrow," adapted from *Antiques Roadshow* website (www.pbs.org/sgbh/pages/roadshow/tips/collection.html); **p. 47**, Exercise 2 based on article in *USA Today*, March 31, 2000; **p. 52**, "Social Issues and Problems for U.S. Teenagers" chart data from *U.S. Crime Statistics*: Monthly average based on an eight-month period (Jan. 1–Sept. 1, 2000) report from www.at-risk.com/cgi/stats.cgi; **pp. 53–54**, Reading One, "Urban Angels," from The Alliance of the Guardian Angels, Inc., Brooklyn, NY; **p. 56**, Reading Two, "Two Real Angels," from The Alliance of the Guardian Angels, Inc., Brooklyn, NY; **p. 75**, Reading Two, "Did You Know," data from Blockbuster, Inc. Blockbuster name, design, and related marks are trademarks of Blockbuster, Inc.; **p. 107**, "Increase in Driving in the United States in the 1990s" bar graph data from U.S. Department of Transportation, Factors Contributing to the Growth in Driving. Travel Behavior Issues in the 90s. Federal Transit Administration, Washington, DC, July 1992, p. 14; **p. 116**, Chart data from The New York Times, Feb. 26, 1997; **p. 123**, "Children Born in the United States 1994–1998" chart data from Centers for Disease Control, Washington, DC; **p. 126**, Reading One, "Seven Tiny Miracles," from *Time* Magazine, Dec. 1, 1997; **p. 129**, Letter from the Dionne quintuplets from *Time* Magazine, Dec. 1, 1997; **p. 141**, New Jersey Lottery pie chart and Pick 6 ticket courtesy of New Jersey State Lottery, Lawrenceville, NJ